Reimagin... Research for Re...
Academy...
Post-Conf...

STUDIES IN INCLUSIVE EDUCATION
Volume 15

Series Editor
Roger Slee, *Institute of Education, University of London, UK.*

Scope
This series addresses the many different forms of exclusion that occur in schooling across a range of international contexts and considers strategies for increasing the inclusion and success of all students. In many school jurisdictions the most reliable predictors of educational failure include poverty, Aboriginality and disability. Traditionally schools have not been pressed to deal with exclusion and failure. Failing students were blamed for their lack of attainment and were either placed in segregated educational settings or encouraged to leave and enter the unskilled labour market. The crisis in the labor market and the call by parents for the inclusion of their children in their neighborhood school has made visible the failure of schools to include all children.

Drawing from a range of researchers and educators from around the world, Studies in Inclusive Education will demonstrate the ways in which schools contribute to the failure of different student identities on the basis of gender, race, language, sexuality, disability, socio-economic status and geographic isolation. This series differs from existing work in inclusive education by expanding the focus from a narrow consideration of what has been traditionally referred to as special educational needs to understand school failure and exclusion in all its forms. Moreover, the series will consider exclusion and inclusion across all sectors of education: early years, elementary and secondary schooling, and higher education.

Reimagining Research for Reclaiming the Academy in Iraq: Identities and Participation in Post-Conflict Enquiry

The Iraq Research Fellowship Programme

Celebrating the 80th anniversary of The Council for Assisting Refugee Academics (CARA)

Edited by

Heather Brunskell-Evans and Michele Moore

SENSE PUBLISHERS
ROTTERDAM/BOSTON/TAIPEI

A C.I.P. record for this book is available from the Library of Congress.

ISBN: 978-94-6091-895-7 (paperback)
ISBN: 978-94-6091-896-4 (hardback)
ISBN: 978-94-6091-897-1 (e-book)

Published by: Sense Publishers,
P.O. Box 21858,
3001 AW Rotterdam,
The Netherlands
https://www.sensepublishers.com/

Printed on acid-free paper

DEDICATION

This book is dedicated to all those academics, their friends and families, who are in need or in exile, wherever they find themselves in the process of reimagining the world in which we live.

It is also dedicated to the young generation of our own families – to Charley and to Eve, and to baby Hugo – with the hope that they will be blessed with the aspiration to help forge a more peaceful future.

TABLE OF CONTENTS

SERIES EDITOR'S PREFACE

Let me declare my interest. Writing a series editor's preface is typically a task performed at a tangible distance. One reads the book or collection of people's chapters and then composes a series of unifying and summarising statements that are often unread as the book travels through the world. My task here is different. I was the *academic coordinator* for the Iraq Research Fellowship Programme (IRFP) and worked closely with the editors and contributors to this text on the programme. So, though I write sitting at a table in a front room of a house in far-away Melbourne, the words are not disinterested nor is there a distance from this project that the geography may suggest.

The IRFP was not just another academic assignment; it was quite different. While engaged on the familiar territory of research infrastructure and productivity, the principal goal was to assist people whose lives and academic work had been wrenched from them by wars, international embargo, ongoing conflict and the relentless struggle of trying to deal with a deep poverty born of the destructive forces of war. Moreover my nationality, for what that is worth these days, is Australian. That fact connects me to Iraq in a relationship of international culpability. The effect of this project was and remains deeply visceral.

The chronology of my involvement with IRFP is interesting. A colleague at the Institute of Education asked me if I would be interested in a project looking at school curriculum in Iraq. Having been responsible for curriculum reform in a large Ministry of Education in Australia, I was interested. That the context was Iraq was intriguing. A meeting was arranged with Kate Robertson from The Council for Assisting Refugee Academics (CARA). Kate brought to the meeting a world of which I had no knowledge beyond highly mediated and inadequate media representations. Dr.Yahya Al-Kubaisi presents the curriculum project in chapter three of this text. The Iraq Research Fellowship Programme provides a mechanism for directing and sustaining support to Iraqi academics, living in Iraq and displaced, to build collaborative projects that are of strategic importance to rebuilding Iraq. This work is fundamental to rebuilding the higher education sector in Iraq.

The logistical challenges were significant as people travelled across sensitive borders to meet and work on the trans-disciplinary projects. For us who travelled from the safety of homes and universities in England, the risks taken by our colleagues from Iraq were breath taking and humbling. This proscribed the relationships that needed to be formed in this work. It was necessary to create a process where external expertise was available to support the work of Iraqi academics and to give them access to recent international developments in their field. As the editors observe this is problematic in a context of enduring post-colonial struggle. Working in different languages further complicates research relationships. Touraine's (2000:195) reflection on working across these tensions is useful:

> In a world of intense cultural exchanges, there can be no democracy unless we recognize the diversity of cultures and the relations of domination that exist between them. The two elements are equally important: we must

recognize the diversity of cultures, but also the existence of cultural domination. ... The struggle for the liberation of cultural minorities can lead to their communitarianization, or in other words their subordination to an authoritarian cultural power.

The programme and workshop processes were profoundly important. At the heart of the work was a need to build sustainable relationships. Moreover the task for those of us coming from outside of the Iraq experience was to offer our knowledge, skills and networks to build the quality and profile of the research. This had to be done in a context where cultural distances and oppressions had been at the heart of the destruction of the Iraqi academy and those who worked therein. The process was iterative and highly contestable. Meetings at the end, very end, of the workshop days were sometimes volatile and the organising group would divide and reform over strategy and points of organisation. Notwithstanding the struggles around strategy and programme, there was an acknowledgement that we were engaged in a project that was much more important and significant than ourselves and we quickly regrouped. The commitment of all participants to the programme was remarkable, as was the sense of collegiality and good will.

This text is an important inclusion in the Studies in Inclusive Education series. The chapters collectively represent a vital response to the destruction of the higher education sector in Iraq and to rebuilding the academy and educational opportunities. This is the heartland of inclusive education.

REFERENCE

Touraine, A. (2000). *Can we live together? Equality and difference.* Cambridge, Polity Press.

Roger Slee
Series Editor
The Victoria Institute for Education, Diversity and Lifelong Learning.

FOREWORD

Iraq, known as Mesopotamia, is home to the oldest civilisation in the world. With a cultural history of more than 10,000 years Iraq is the Cradle of Civilization which is easily reflected in the people's persistent resilience. It is after all the land which has experience wide range of extremes including wars, dictatorships, sanctions and occupations. Since the creation of modern Iraq in 1931, education has played an important role in developing the society and in capacity building. However, some of the education policies unfortunately have created tensions rather than integration. For example, the schools curriculum was built on the base of the identity of the Sunni State, with an attempt to address ethnic and sectarian nature of the Iraqi society but that did not succeed and as a result, a lot of conflict was created in the modern education system.

Until the beginning of the seventies, the academic activities in Iraq were still in its (relatively) normal evolving period. Iraq academy as part of the intellectual activities was reasonably free from any political ideology. However, after the coup of 1968 which brought the Baath Party to power, the political ideology started to dominate and control all aspects of social life and academic activities. The dominance of the political ideology caused many serious problems to science and higher education. After 1980 and the Iran-Iraq war, the domination of the ideology was further affecting in the tendency of militarizing the society, and the intense focusing on the military research and development programmes. Additionally, the invasion of Kuwait and the subsequent Gulf war as well as the economical sanctions all led to the education in Iraq to suffer greatly and lag behind significantly. These periods were marked by: limited social, political and intellectual freedom; little or no connections with the international educational and scientific community; low standards of scientific journals; little or no contributions to international science activities including conferences and journals; little or no financial support for non-military activities; no internet or access to computers, new text books or other publications, among many other difficulties which limited the development and the progress of Iraqi higher education.

Additionally, there was the dictatorship and the oppressive nature of the regime, which meant that many academics were executed or disappeared forever because of their political views. Examples of this include the execution of the distinguished scholar and author Mohamed Baqer Al-Sader, who refused to support the regime, and the thirteen year imprisonment of nuclear scientist Dr Hussain Al-Shahristani for refusing to work on Saddam's nuclear programme.

The situation after the 2003 occupation has been dramatically different. The extent of the suffering and the difficulties is indiscriminate. Iraq has been bombed and systematically destroyed more than any country in the world, and the Iraqi people have probably suffered more than any other people in the world. The main concerns for post 2003 conflict are personal safety and security.

The situation for higher education is no better after 2003 and this book illustrates, with many heartfelt examples, the difficulties and challenges that Iraq higher education and Iraqi academics have faced since. It may be true to say that no students elsewhere in the world are searched for bombs or guns before entering exam rooms, expect in Iraq! This is what the President of Baghdad University told me about their experience in 2004, when the University academic staff were conducting the exams for more than 70,000 students with Baghdad in a state of war, with little or no security presence at the University. He also told me that it was their nightmare scenario that one of the discontented students unhappy with their exam might raise a false bomb alarm disrupting the whole exam proceedings! Luckily nothing of that had happened and the exams were successfully and smoothly conducted!

This book, titled *Reimagining Research for Reclaiming the Academy in Iraq: Identities and Participation in Post-Conflict Enquiry*, edited eloquently by two distinguished British academics to celebrate the 80th anniversary of the Council for Assisting Refugee Academics (CARA), focuses on the Iraq Research Fellowship Programme (IRFP). It contains a wealth of information on Iraq academy since the 2003 occupation. With chapters written by Iraqi academics who took part in IRFP and reflected on their own experiences, the books has contributions from social and natural scientists as well as medics. It covers topics as wide as gender studies, curriculum studies in post-invasion Iraq, difficulties and challenges in setting up research in post conflict conditions highlighting the people's resilience to complete experiments regardless of institutional electrical supply, by taking samples home to domestic fridge and later processed on kitchen tables. Difficulties in training paediatricians working with children affected by conflict in Iraq, and the experience of conducting research on diagnosis of tuberculosis in Iraq are also well covered. A joint project involving many researchers from Iraq shows the valuable role and work of CARA in supporting academics who are displaced or affected by post-conflict situation. I strongly recommend this publication to the widest possible audience.

Adel Sharif
Professor of Water Engineering and Process Innovation
University of Surrey

ACKNOWLEDGEMENTS

The production of this book represents a period of sharing and research collaboration that began in the winter of 2009 when the first meeting of the Iraq Research Fellowship Programme (IRFP), sponsored by The Council for Assisting Refugee Academics (CARA) was held in Amman, Jordan. Hopefully these collaborations, the social networks and personal and professional relationships (including a much celebrated wedding!) which were generated through the programme will endure.

This book is a collective effort which emerged through critical and uncertain discussions that took place during and between bi-annual IRFP workshops. We owe a debt of enormous gratitude to CARA for its funding of the IRFP and enabling the critical and reflective conversations that have made their way in to the pages of this book, about ways in which research can contribute to the rebuilding of social capital in Iraq, to take place. Thanks are owed to wider programme funders including The Open Society Institute and the Sigrid Rausing Trust and to those who have contributed time as IRFP Committee Members. The vision of Kate Robertson, Deputy Executive Secretary of CARA and the Iraq Programme Manager has been compelling for all and we thank her for inspiration and unrelenting energy. The courage of Iraqi scholars who have been involved in the IRFP provides testimony to the immense possibilities for rebuilding the academy as part of the project of rebuilding Iraq and those of us who have contributed from safer places in the world have been privileged to come to know them, work with them, listen, learn and write with them.

Sincere thanks are conveyed to all the contributors, who were willing to push the boundaries of their familiar writing practices as part of the process of cooperating on this book.

Throughout the editing of the book, our families have been immensely supportive and for this we extend our heartfelt thanks.

MICHELE MOORE AND HEATHER BRUNSKELL-EVANS

NOBEL PRIZES FOR IRAQI RESEARCHERS?

INTRODUCTION

This book focuses on the work of The Council for Assisting Refugee Academics (CARA) in particular, the work of one of its contemporary branches, the Iraq Research Fellowship Programme (IRFP). Through the IRFP CARA has worked to support the academic freedom of Iraqi scholars at risk of oppression and exclusion from the academy. The book is located as one of a number of events and publications to mark CARA's eightieth year. It is written particularly to celebrate the achievement of twelve teams of Iraqi research scholars who have sought support, knowing as they first came together in 2009 that *'working as an academic in Iraq is a hazardous occupation'*. In the words of those scholars: *'the value of the IRFP is worth its weight in gold. I come to [the IRFP] to learn about research ... I see hope'; 'we listen to each other, we try to understand each other and we hope new waves of amnesty will come in to our research and our lives'*. A central purpose of the book is to provide a forum for Iraqi scholars to voice their own experiences in relation to the IRFP. It is widely accepted that the current situation of Iraqi academics 'provides a much-needed reminder that intellectual freedom must not be taken for granted' (Nature, Editorial, 2010).

CARA launched an Iraq Programme in late 2006 at the height of an Iraqi assassination campaign against academics. Numerous scholars fled from Iraq and dispersed into different countries, in particular neighbouring Jordan. Decimation of the academy in Iraq, which had begun long before 2006 following UN sanctions, lack of investment and failure to protect universities during periods of conflict, was endemic. A disabling of the individual research of scholars and academic teams ensued. The IRFP was launched in 2009 when changing security in Iraq offered up the possibility of working with those still in post in Iraq and reconnecting those still in exile. Thus, the IRFP was conceived to help reverse the trend of academic annihilation and contribute to the resurgence of Iraq's Higher Education (HE) sector. In this book scholars who have been both directly and indirectly involved with the IRFP share their experience of research opportunities afforded to them by CARA. They explore the challenges, excitements and achievements of the work they have contributed through their enquiries to the rebuilding of academy in Iraq.

The chapters in this book all reflect personal journeys undertaken in the context of collective research engagements. They embody and produce a commitment to the possibilities of rebuilding both academy and community through shared research endeavours. But they also evidence the complexity of producing, writing

H. Brunskell-Evans & M. Moore (Eds.), Reimagining Research for Reclaiming the Academy in Iraq: Identities and Participation in Post-Conflict Enquiry: The Iraq Research Fellowship Programme, 1–15.

about and disseminating projects when research activities are entangled in vivid and dangerous tensions associated with an environment described as 'post' conflict yet in which, post the initial toppling of the regime, the opposite is the case and conflict still reigns; *'there are still clashes and skirmishes and it isn't always possible to go out... then clashes seem to die down. But later we hear gunfire again somewhere in the city and it is not always easy to go to the university'* ... *'all night recently there have been firing sounds, big and small explosions. I don't sleep. In the morning I cannot think'.* It is well known that conflict is not a thing of the past in contemporary Iraq and that living conditions will continue to be perilous (Marfleet and Chatty, 2003). The Higher Education system in Iraq is still characterised by 'murder, destruction, corruption and decline' (Adriaensens, 2011).

It is in the challenge of re-imagining both the nature and power of research in the re-construction of post-conflict Iraq that we find spaces for new emergent dialogue, knowledge production, agency and prospects for re-building the academy according to the priorities of Iraqi scholars and people and scope for new conversations about research controversies and contentions more generally. It is to the unfolding of such a journey and the lessons learned through making it, which eighty years of the work of CARA has assisted , that this book turns. The book draws together a collection of reflections written by and with Iraqi 'refugee' academics who, in the aftermath of the Anglo-American invasion in April 2003, describe the processes involved in re-imagining and re-building their research, and through that process attempt to re-claim the Academy in Iraq.

Projects funded through the IRFP are outlined below. The stories of the first six listed became the direct focus of this book:

- Use of Molecular Methods for Better Understanding of Tuberculosis in Iraq
- Transforming the Learning Environment through Theatre (TLET): Developing a Basra model
- Female Iraqi Academics in Post-Invasion Iraq: Roles, Challenges & Capacities
- Analytical Study of Curricula of Education in Iraq
- Mobile Phone Technologies to Enhance Self-Management & Education for Iraqi Diabetics
- Child Health in Iraqi Higher Education: Needs assessment for psychosocial training

Elements of six further IRFP projects have been drawn on in places throughout the book to provide further amplification or enable fresh illustration of points under discussion. These projects are:

- Potential use of Trees in Phytoremediation and Phytostabilisation of Heavy Metals in Iraq
- Transfer of Expertise in NMR Spectroscopy from the University of Liverpool to Iraq
- Upgrading of historical areas in Iraqi cities: reviewing the utility of space syntax in Baghdad
- A comparative study of the genetics of Behcets disease in Iraq

- Assessment of the primary healthcare system in Iraq using a multimodal method
- Design and synthesis of wide band fractal antennas for on-body communications using method-of-moments.

As Editors we are two women academics teaching and researching in UK universities with direct knowledge of the IRFP since each of us has worked on the programme from 2009 till the present. We are, of course, acutely aware of the limitations of our own outsider insights and perspectives into the IRFP. Critical questions need continually to be asked about the centrality of Western academic approaches in the IRFP, including in the compilation and production of this book. The medium of English as the language of IRFP scholarship obviously imposes particular power relations and tensions upon research activities and outputs, shaping the collated personal narratives gathered together for the book in particular ways. Some chapters, or sections of chapters, were first written in Arabic for example and their fluency has been compromised by translation into English. We have deliberately left moments of uncertain translation untouched where these do not devalue the content of what the writer is saying. Such moments convey the enormity of the task faced by Iraqi scholars seeking to engage with CARA's wish for their academic work to hold up within an international – predominantly English language – academic audience. They also give insight in to the capacity building role and tremendous achievement of the IRFP. And so, in line with other literature concerning authentic representation of voice in research, we have not sought to smooth out difficulties relating to language and communication but to reveal these and ask the reader to consider them (Moore, 2000; Clough, 2010).

To bring the book to life and give the research projects a human face, many contributors have excavated personal collections of notes from IRFP meetings to capture emergent images, moments of clarity or conversely confusion, impressions of shifting ideas, emotional responses and changing sentiments. All who have done so have no sense of the 'validity' of their considerations but know that these details elucidate something very real about developing research in Iraq in that they demonstrate the strength and force of Iraqi resilience. This certainly means that not all of the material in this book makes for easy and comfortable reading. We have had to work carefully with the genuine anxiety that inclusion of personal voices brings a possible danger of exposing vulnerable people, of creating ambiguity or of 'telling tales out of school' for which there will be repercussions. However, for many contributors recollected conversations, scribbles in a diary or extracts from systematically garnered field notes help give a backdrop to their research accounts which make up the main part of this book. The research accounts presented are therefore not confined to descriptions of knowledge production, but express in personal detail the minutiae of processes of enquiry that have evolved throughout the IRFP years within the political context of HE in Iraq. As Editors we ask the reader to reflect upon these details as we believe it to be in these minutiae that we might touch upon possibilities for change, creativity and wisdom and for resistance and hope that will enable the rebuilding of the academy in Iraq.

COUNCIL FOR ASSISTING REFUGEE ACADEMICS (CARA)

CARA was initiated in the 1930s to foster the work of refugee academics fleeing persecution from fascist regimes (Seabrook 2009; see also http://www.academic-refugees.org). It was originally called the Academic Assistance Council and was founded to assist Jewish academics dismissed by the Nazis from German universities who were threatened with expulsion from Germany or worse. Whilst the organization was originally seen as a temporary arrangement, Seabrook (2009) draws our attention to the fact that sadly, the need it sought to meet persists three generations later. CARA's work, both past and present, has encountered a great deal of resistance, both official and popular, since its overarching concern is for the fate of educated, often socially committed, economically active and politically involved people in their country of origin. In the current political climate, in which to be a refugee or an asylum seeker is perhaps to be vilified, CARA defends the contribution, over the past 75 years of academic refugees to Britain's social, intellectual, economic and cultural life. Indeed, Seabrook (2009) argues, intellectual and cultural capacity often explains why academics suffer: they are targeted or singled out by ideologically driven regimes as 'threats' to that regime's maintenance and stability. This is the lived experience of the Iraqi scholars who have contributed to this book.

CONTEXT OF THE IRAQI RESEARCH FELLOWSHIP PROGRAMME (IRFP)

CARA's mandate for support of academics was inherited from its predecessors, The Society for the Protection of Science and Learning, *'to ensure their special knowledge and abilities may continue to be used for the benefit of mankind'*. Until the present moment in world politics CARA supported the refugee academic externally to the country from which asylum was sought. Arguably, the term 'refugee' is unhelpful. Under current international law it requires the individual concerned to have crossed their national border, that is, to be outside of their country of origin. When the Society for the Protection of Science and Learning was incorporated in 1959 Articles describe 'refugee' to mean *'a person who has left his country or his occupation as a result of political, racial or religious oppression or discrimination or the fear of such oppression or discrimination'*; that is to say, they do not have to have left their country. The focus is much more on their continued contribution to mankind, such as their ability to fulfill their role as academics and educators. The IRFP (http://www.academic-refugees.org/Iraq-Programme.asp) is situated differently and is unique in the history of CARA since its mandate is sustaining the academic capital of HE in Iraq itself. The first level aims of the IRFP are *'to enhance regional and Iraqi research and teaching capacities; to undertake and deliver innovative research outputs of relevance to Iraq's future; to nurture lasting international research collaborations and to reengage selected Iraqi academics in exile'*. There is a tension here which remains unresolved and to which we return in the final chapter of the book: sustaining scholars in their academic environment involves the necessity for some of the academics in the research projects to which they are attached to be classified as refugees before they can apply for funding from CARA. Refugee status can take a long time to acquire; and the scholars themselves eschew the term 'refugee' since they don't consider themselves to be refugees but rather as post-2003 invasion exiles who go back and forth to Iraq; in reality not all are able to go back and forth and some must adopt different persona depending on who they are talking to. For this reason, the term 'refugee' is not used within the IRFP. The term 'exile' is used so that there is no refugee requirement placed on the Iraq Programme. CARA accepted at the launch of the Iraq Programme in 2006 that Iraqi academics were being targeted as a group so that the first activities, namely a Hardship Fund and UK Fellowship Scheme were available to all Iraqi academics, inside or outside of Iraq. Szenasi (2010) places emphasis on seeking to understand 'refugee' identities from the perspectives of those so-labelled in order to connect knowledge and power discourses that have greatest potential to contribute towards developing justice. This is a tension which the IRFP fully recognises.

Baker, Ismael and Ismael (2009) provide a social description and political analysis of the cultural cleansing, the looting of museums, the burning of libraries and the murder of academics in Iraq in the years following the Occupation by the United States and Coalition forces. Fuller and Adriaensens (2009) elaborate on one specific aspect of this, namely the killing of Iraqi scholars and intellectuals and the decimation of the academy. They argue that of the many tragedies that have be-fallen Iraqi society since 2003, 'one of the most heinous and overlooked' is that of the 'elimination of hundreds or thousands of Iraqi academics' (2009: 149). In the words of IRFP scholars *'there have been terrible losses'*. Another explained *'key members of our research teams have been assassinated. This creates a feeling of darkness'*.

Although the killings of academics in the aftermath of the invasion took place within the broad context of attacks against Iraq's professional classes, and thus the plight of academics is not to be understood in isolation but as a lens through which to view the wider horror that afflicted occupied Iraq, the questions of who has been killed, how or even why, have not been substantively addressed (Fuller and Adriaensens, 2009). The height of the assassination campaign was 2006, and although Basra, Mosul and other Iraqi universities witnessed a substantial number of killings the majority of murders took place within the various HE colleges and institutions in Baghdad, especially Baghdad University itself. Fuller and Adriaensens (2009) point out that the high level of murder at the universities of these three cities does not correspond with the overall levels of violence in their respective provinces, and they conjecture that it reflects the leading position of these universities, as well as the potential role of these latter as capitals in an Iraq divided along major ethno-sectarian lines. There was general agreement at the first IRFP meeting in Jordan also in 2009, when one Iraqi scholar told those listening *'I am glad CARA have invited us. But for all of us Iraqis here, we have taken many risks to take part'*.

In the wake of targeted assassinations, Fuller and Adriaensens (op cit) have also described as explicit an implicit threat of assassination familiar to IRFP participants; always somebody to be heard wondering *'I have not heard anything from the other two scholars which is worrying ...'* and further along the corridor *'no word from Anees yet ... I hope everything is okay with him'.* As with targeted assassinations, there is very little evidence of who is directly responsible for issuing the various forms of intimidation, but like the murders themselves, threats and intimidation have become a widespread phenomenon. The explicit messages and demand contained within the threats serve two functions, both of which are underlined by the actual violence: the first is to hound academics out of their social roles, their homes, and frequently their homeland; the second is to ensure that all those academics who remain in Iraq, whether or not they are the immediate object of death threats, exist within a pervasive culture of fear in which they are encouraged to seek refuge abroad or to relocate within the country, effectively becoming internally displaced *'I feel uncomfortable if I disagree with my colleagues'.* There is apprehension, *'I don't trust. I fear'.* Abiding horror stifles academic participation, *'my mother used to be a Professor but she will not leave the house now. She cannot pass through our front door since my brother was killed right in front of it'.*

The climate of fear in universities is exacerbated by the rise of religious fundamentalism. Where the academy in Iraq before the Occupation had been secular, representing a backbone of the nation in the face of potential partition along ethno-sectarian lines suppressed by the previous regime, powerful factions emerged out of the political vacuum opened up by the demolition of the previous political regime. One of the manifestations of the unleashing of sectarian violence was the demands issued by anonymous or unknown groups for students to be segregated by gender and for the institution to stop teaching 'Western ideals' (Fuller and Adriaensens 2009). All of these experiences have been encountered by the researchers whose work the reader will come to engage with through the pages of this book, as a short illustration puts across:

> *In conversations with one of the researchers in Basra about personal and safety issues for our research meeting it sounded like something from a carefully crafted movie plot with lots of secrecy. Security would be enhanced by keeping a very low profile, in moving to a safe sanctuary with no-one knowing who we are or what we are doing. The risks would be in moving about. Apparently the campus is safer.*

With regard to the particularity of this research team's work, *'given what has happened to [the Principal Investigator's] home, with the hand grenade being thrown, I formulated the opinion that the research meeting would not be safe and so declined the invitation'.*

Whatever one's own views of the invasion of Iraq and of regime change, the reality is that numerous scholars fled from Iraq and dispersed into different countries, in particular neighbouring Jordan. The carving out of an apolitical, independent and neutral space in which CARA can continue to operate, driven solely by academic considerations, is delicate and deeply contentious in an extremely polarized environment.

IRFP PROJECTS

By 2009 the IRFP was up and running and ready to receive its first round of research teams. As articulated in the earlier description of 'first level' activities, the IRFP encompasses a number of complementary activities responding to the following objectives: to fund research projects which facilitate the well-being and re-building of Iraqi society; to re-engage with and enhance the research and teaching capacities of recent exiles and those academics still working in Iraq; and to foster international collaboration opportunities At the time of writing in 2011 the IRFP has facilitated the twelve research projects listed at the start of this chapter with further projects under negotiation, subject to future funding. Each project team consists of Iraqi Research Fellows, typically two early- to mid-career Iraqi academics in post in Iraq, and an Iraqi academic in exile, for example in the UK, Canada or Jordan. Western academics, reflecting CARA's connections rather than who would be eligible to be involved, work for the IRFP voluntarily, and they occupy one of two possible positions: one is that of the Principal Investigator (PI) and another is that of Facilitator. The role of the English speaking, usually Western PI with professorial status typically based in the UK, is to ensure that the team meets its objectives, international standards, budget and time-lines. It is assumed that PIs bring international academic experience to the table in this collaboration. In addition, each team is supported by an English speaking Western academic who takes the role of Facilitator and works both with and across research teams in response to needs and requirements articulated by the team and embedded in the wider programme aims. The Facilitators ensure, in consultation with all team members, that mentoring is productive, that Research Fellows are consulted about their perspectives of the programme, and that the group dynamics are supportive both to individuals and conducive to the larger IRFP aims. It is true however, that when the IRFP began, Western academic contributors travelling to the first meeting in Amman knew little about the predicaments of Iraqi scholars, 'we on the outside – had hardly any sense of what was going on when we first went to Jordan and little sense of how the war in Iraq affected the daily lives of Iraqi academics'.

In the context of these starting points, research projects have had to be operationalised across many very different and culturally diverse university settings, often thousands of miles apart. There is only one team, working on extraction of heavy metals from uranium contaminated soils, in which all of the Iraqi scholars are effectively hosted in the UK for the major part of their project. In all other cases workshops were convened to allow the teams to meet every four months in Jordan to avoid security pressures in Iraq and circumvent visa restrictions for people in exile. All projects contend with technical challenges and ongoing disruption due to fragile infrastructure in a post-conflict country. Poor broadband connectivity for example, compromises email contact and all teams report seemingly endless material, environmental and attitudinal obstacles to their research in Iraq. The day to day lived reality of barely tolerable conditions experienced by academics in contemporary post-conflict Iraq have been vividly detailed elsewhere (Rowlatt and Witwit, 2010). Accounts of curtailed academic freedoms are not new. The accounts of IRFP scholars assembled for this book reaffirm the critical imperative for keeping CARAs work alive. They show how CARA continues to assist academics in need to rebuild their lives in practical ways. And how, through this assistance, commitment to academia is fortified which enables academics who live with fear to develop new knowledge, forge new networks and capacities to drive forward their aspiration to *'condemn violence, to live quietly'*; *'what we are trying to discover through our research is only one part of our work, we want our research to restore peace'*. IRFP project teams are only at the beginning of a process of re-imaging research for a reimagined Iraq but they will frame a contribution to the next generation and play a vital role in shaping society as Iraq's educators.

Despite multiple barriers to research in post-conflict Iraq, powerful projects are being carried out through the IRFP. Many have reached the stage of both national and international dissemination with publications in print or pending. A number of teams are responding to a Call for Papers for a Special Issue in 2013 of the journal *Medicine, Conflict and Survival* (originally published under the title of Medicine and War) a world leading peer-reviewed international journal for all those interested in health aspects of violence and human rights. A forthcoming Special Issue of *Al-Raida,* an interdisciplinary peer-reviewed journal published twice yearly by the Institute for Women's Studies in the Arab World at the Lebanese American University, on women & disability in the Arab World emerges directly from regional collaborations inspired by an Iraq Research Fellowship Programme project. Although IRFP projects are each concerned with specific academic sites of research, unity is to be found between the diverse research teams in that they all contend with the incontrovertible externally observable effect on their work of the current political situation of post-conflict Iraq.

CHALLENGES FACING IRFP RESEARCH TEAMS

The connections across experience for IRFP scholars remind us that research does not occur in an academic vacuum but is always an activity located within a complex set of relational, situational, cultural and political conditions (Tuhiwai Smith, 2002; Lavia and Moore, 2011).The actual nature of these conditions remain largely impenetrable, certainly unfathomable, to scholars working in the relatively protected context of the Western academy. The circumstances of IRFP microbiologists, for example, are chastening. They struggled tirelessly to overcome problems of live cough sample transportation through road blocks. Travelling to Baghdad to buy materials important for their work routinely ended in meeting another road blocked or encounters at check-points which prevented visits to suppliers. There was nothing to do but return day after day to try to get supplies but meanwhile the clock ticked away and precious samples deteriorate in unrelenting heat of the day. Their samples required refrigeration and so, as no electricity was available in their university until 4pm, researchers had to take samples home to the domestic fridge and later process them on the kitchen table to avoid risk of incomplete experiments.

Research teams studying social awareness and social change encountered daily powerful control political and religious parties exerted on the environment of the University. In such circumstances where interference, usually with violence, from religious parties and militias has been an inescapable issue, research has had to proceed with much caution. Our colleagues said *'sometimes we prefer to keep quiet and keep low profile so that we don't face danger'*. We have had to take on board this message to help locate the tone of this book.

Women researchers have had to find creative ways to circumvent obstacles to their participation in the IRFP presented by colleagues who believe male academics should be privileged to take up such opportunities. When first presenting their work at an IRFP meeting some women were warned by an observer not to underestimate extremism or to neglect *'a wider trend towards social conservatism of people who want to backward the women in Iraq'*. Rowlatt and Witwit (op cit) have described the need for Iraqi female academics to sometimes operate or travel in clandestine ways to pursue their research interests. In addition to workplace barriers to participation in academic life, Iraqi women involved with IRFP juggled their research work with multiple family commitments – as do academics who are parents world over – but carrying an additional mantle of fear; thinking about research with dread in the heart as described on one memorable occasion by a researcher who had left her child at home in a city where a bomb exploded only days before near to the child's school picnic. Researchers studying policy issues find workers in Iraq too afraid to be interviewed. On more than one occasion, having completed a rare interview, text messages from interviewees tipped off by friendly colleagues, warned respondents they were deemed to have caused offense, to have conducted politically dangerous conversations and the researcher was urged immediately to seek hiding. Working in an internet café brings risk as there is ongoing uncertainty over restricted and non-restricted websites and partisan interpretation of acceptable enquiry. A social science researcher downloading a picture of Bill Clinton shaking the hand of an Iraqi government minister at Harvard told how *'the police came to my colleague and put a hand on his shoulder and said 'don't you know it is illegal?''*. The first meeting of the Soils Contamination team imploded when researchers on the road from Iraq failed to arrive amidst rumours of targeted persecution and then kidnapping. Sudden disappearance of colleagues is familiar to all of the teams. An Iraqi scholar noted *'there should be a Nobel Prize awarded to Iraqi researchers for working in such conditions'*.

Perhaps it is in response to the shifting tensions embedded in the unchartered landscape of research in post-conflict Iraq that each of the research teams is dynamic, transforming academic and professional communities. Even while projects are not yet finished, they are contributing research data and evolving research practice in ways which impact on the international academic scene. The work of the TB team is known beyond small research communities in Iraq, now having important links with the World Health Organisation and with the STOP TB global campaign which aims to save a million lives by 2015. Similarly the work of the team studying gender issues has crossed boundaries of global academic and professional significance. Work on strategies for managing diabetes in Iraq has culminated in discussions of regional importance showing the strength and influence of research and education links forged through the IRFP.

When the IRFP began in 2009 tension was evident in the first meeting which was not only the product of the collective heightened expectations, hopes, and dreams, and of differential views about how to carry out research. There was clear personal wariness between Iraqi scholars arising perhaps from knowledge of each other's political affiliation as these were defined along sectarian lines in post–invasion Iraq. What we have discovered by working on the IRFP is that the response of the Iraqi academics to the Western invasion is complex and sometimes divided. Some scholars have claimed, tentatively in the presence of Editors, the invasion was a neo-colonial act, namely the Western occupation of a sovereign territory for its own purposes; others have put forward its benefits in terms of the freedoms afforded by the imposition of normative liberal values. On the whole all Iraqi scholars, at least overtly, accept the authority of Western academics belonging to the CARA. The assumption is made, rightly or wrongly, that Western academics bring knowledge and experience to expedite reengagement, such as familiarity with 'how to publish internationally' or 'how to ensure your research is rigorous within the terms of its field'.

Throughout the chapters which now follow, we wish to be mindful of the huge distance between research and academic lives with which scholars in Iraq and scholars in the West contend. These can be glimpsed even in the most elementary exchanges about how a UK university will authorise a mode of purchase and payment for essential equipment:

Dear All,

Just to clarify, the accounts people here will not release our funds unless they have the proper paperwork. This consists of a formal estimate/quote before the order is placed and a receipt for it after it is placed. For laptops they prefer you to buy from places who will support the equipment by way of a receipt and a guarantee.

Dear Dr,

The steps which you are talking about for purchasing laptops are probably what that are in the UK. Here in Iraq we cannot find such a facility. Here purchasing has to be achieved from markets directly by people who want to buy.

And then later,

Dear Dr,

I would like to inform you that in Iraq we cannot easily find the computer programme but we can easily find a cracked version of C++, then do the required calculations, however I do not know whether the calculations can then be used for our project in view of putting the achieved results in an international journal or conference. If we can use the cracked version then we can go ahead but we do not have a way to buy from a supplier formally'

Hello All,

No, we cannot use a cracked version.

A friendly expression of care between colleagues summarizes challenges facing IRFP research teams: *'best wishes for your research ... be careful out there and watch your back'.*

CHAPTERS FROM IRFP TEAMS

What will be found in the following chapters is a collection of personal reflections by Iraqi academics on experience of participation in the IRFP, testimonies which reveal an appreciation of the strenuous efforts made by all involved to take forward the complicated problem of revitalising research in the Iraqi academy. The chapters are steeped in what participants in the IRFP were seeing and thinking and hearing during the two years or so which they spent on the project. They provide a record and analysis of the processes which took place, between 2009–2011, in facilitating and in developing projects within the IRFP which were designed to help pave the way for the rebuilding of the academy in Iraq. The chapters show unerring commitment to research and to research freedom in the context of post-conflict Iraq.

When the idea of a collectively produced book was first mooted it had seemed barely possible that researchers writing about such diverse spheres of intellectual activity as, for example, 'community theatre' in contrast with 'diagnosis of tuberculosis', might share a platform of commentary on their experience of the IRFP. There were two schools of thought in the early days of the IRFP–on the one hand those who felt it impossible to pursue generic research strategy across disciplines and on the other those who were looking to encourage the cross fertilization. These perspectives were held together by CARA's overriding commitment to privileging the development of research that could *make a difference to Iraq*. It soon became clear, as very different research teams struggled to find a co-operative mode of working together, that recurring themes, to do with identities and participation in post-conflict enquiry operated as overarching, exciting and unifying points of deep interest.

To respond to these interests, and to enable the project of shared writing which has ultimately led to this book, CARA funded a Writing Workshop held also in Amman, to which teams indicating an interest in, and readiness for, reflecting and writing together were invited. The book writing process began in a spirit of open mystification, with ready acknowledgement that contributors from different cultural worlds, and divergent worlds of scholarship, would feel uncertain about how to approach the task of shared writing. In the workshop we set out to build on our differences, to exploit the existing wealth of contrasting expertise amongst us, so that participants mentored each other as writers of the chapters that now form the basis of this book. Through plenary sessions, team based workshops, independent writing time, peer review work in small groups and individual tutorials, research teams began to work on specific parts of their chapter (such as the beginning, the key arguments, the conclusions they wished todraw). Chapter authors were able to benefit from focussed discussions with their own project team members but also from feedback on their writing plans from the wider group of contributors, thus benefiting from a range of different world views and perspectives on research, on writing and on experience of the IRFP. Our shared motivation was to get the work of the Iraqi scholars in to print and to show case the critical role CARA had played in enabling the production of their work.

The central questions posed to offer a coherent conceptual framework for the book were: 'What has actually been involved in your efforts to work collaboratively on research projects intended to help rebuild the academy in post-conflict Iraq and what are the implications of this?' 'What do we mean in theoretical and practical terms by the idea of 'collaborative research in a post-conflict setting?' 'Why is reflection on our varied experiences of developing research to support the rebuilding of academy in Iraq important?''What are the possibilities offered by our work for future collaborative research endeavours seeking to regenerate academic life in contexts moving beyond conflict?' 'What is the link between our research endeavours, the development of academic life and rebuilding of a post-conflict society?' 'To what extent is this link central to the rebuilding of Iraq?'

During the course of the IRFP it had become plain to all that these questions could not be considered lightly. Rather, they had come to determine the utility of our shared endeavours over the years, to signify the enormity of difficult conversations which traversed cultural, personal, political and disciplinary boundaries and had led each and every participant to challenge previously held assumptions about the process of research, the production of research knowledge and social transformation. Coming together in a project of shared writing was a challenging undertaking but it enabled recognition that the unlikely synergies of research collaboration made possible through the IRFP forged new communities of research practice that will be central to those who are concerned with histories and experiences of exclusion and oppression encountered in communities and societies almost, but not quite, destroyed by conflict and war. Each chapter addresses some or all of these questions through discourses that are reflective of the specific context/s in which the researchers are working. As Editors we have sometimes intervened to make use of English accessible to the international reader but, as already made clear, we have taken great care not to lose the quality of original voice which pervades the writing.

In the first of the chapters from research teams Mohanad Ahmed, Hassan, Suhad Ahmed, Ali Al-Zaag and Michael Barer discuss their efforts to conduct research on diagnosis of tuberculosis in Iraq. They knew that tuberculosis research, as similarly with research studies of malaria, does have a history of being conducted in unstable environments and so chose appropriate research technologies as part of their research design to accommodate context variables. Nonetheless they describe how they soon felt themselves to be 'trapped in an endless circles' as never-ending bureaucratic and institutional barriers were put in front of them. Their project has achieved huge success, much against the odds, growing from a time when Mohanad and Suhad Ahmed saw themselves as medical researchers destined to remain isolated from the rest of the world and decided to spend their house-keeping on getting research trials started without any connection to a like-minded academic community. Nowadays their research findings have come to the attention of the World Health Organization, they are able to discuss sustainability of their enquiries within Iraq and they are foremost advocates of new modes of research-led teaching within the medical schools of the Iraqi higher education sector.

In the next chapter, Amir Al-Azraki, Nadia Sekran, Michael Pomerantz and Bruce Wooding seek to understand and illustrate conflicts between Iraqi and non-Iraqi perspectives which impact on implementation of new strategies for teaching and learning in the context of Higher Education. They take Forum Theatre as a vehicle for potentially developing self-expression and self-determination within the academy but encounter what appear to be multiple sources of resistance to the possibilities of their project for transformation and change. The chapter develops ideas on ways of understanding this resistance and recognizes the profound cultural conflicts and perceptions on which research is based, with important consequences for development education.

In Chapter Three, Nadje Al-Ali, Huda Al-Dujaili, Inass Al-Enezy and Irada Al-Jeboury draw attention to the difficulties facing female academics in the context of Higher Education in Iraq and the double jeopardy facing women academics seeking to develop new approaches to research with regard to the collection of qualitative data. They challenge the existing value attached to quantitative approaches to research in Iraq persisting in pioneering qualitative research practice in a context in which their methodologies are often viewed as inadequate or even 'un-scientific'. Through presentation of personal narrative in the main body of the chapter they affirm the potentially transformative role of female academics in the endeavor to renegotiate assumptions about scholarship in Iraq and for constructing new ones through raising the seldom heard voices of female Iraqi academics.

In Chapter Four Yahya Al-Kubaisi unravels many apparent contradictions and controversies that have characterised his journey as a researcher of school curriculum in Iraq. He discusses intensely problematic boundaries between academic and political activity which have been thrown into sharp relief through his focus on schools as social institutions which is pointing out more and more directly how, within school curriculum, pedagogy, assessment and the culture of schools messages are conveyed about the kind of society we want. He views research as an immensely important resource for understanding the relationship between schools and society but has suffered many setbacks as the visibility and power of his research has begun to increase. In the context of Iraq, in which governance of schools has been deeply disrupted during episodes of war and conflict, curriculum matters and Yahya Al-Kubaisi's work gets to grips with this in important ways.

Abdul Kareem Al-Obaidi, Ali Ghazi Kamees and Tim Corcoran develop a discussion in Chapter Five about the urgently needed, complex and yet uncharted field of training for paediatricians involved in working with children affected by conflict in Iraq. They each use their personal and professional experience of research and practice in differing cultural contexts of troubled children's lives to explore the issue of sufficiency in terms of paediatric training in Iraq but also to extrapolate understanding of the relationship between insightful research and intervention, children's well being and development and the future development of Iraq.

In Chapter Six, the difficulties of setting up research in conditions shaped by the continuing and long-lasting realities of war have required Alaa Musa Khuttar, Karim Al-Jeboury and Kevin McDonald to rethink major points of practice concerning ethical, methodological and practical dimensions of enquiry. Drawing on their experiences of developing research using new technologies to respond to the urgent health crisis of diabetes, they discuss their attempts to build new modes of research intervention through a series of complex cross-cultural collaborations. They have had to actively grapple with the protractedness of obstacles facing researchers in post-conflict Iraq but have managed to forge new pathways for research with potential to generate durable new solutions for health management.

MOVING ON

As IRFP Facilitators our initial involvement was inspired by huge optimism and the desire to contribute, in however small a measure, to healing the devastation to the Iraqi Academy which we felt our own government's actions had helped cause. Our optimism has subsequently been tempered by the academic and political obstacles and challenges which our Iraqi academic scholars eloquently portray in the following chapters. Iraqi fellows still tell us 'the scholar is an easy target' because 'if a scholar is assassinated it means something in terms of reactions from others'. Through the book we hope to expose some of these difficulties as part of a process through which oppression and marginalization of academics in Iraq – or researchers in situations of conflict anywhere in the world – are resisted. We recognise there is no room for complacency:

> And we leave Jordan ... I got to the UK just fine and only a little late. Where I live in England there is snow and home looks just like a Christmas card (PI, December 2010)here there are still suicide bombers and people injured in attacks. We are sitting in a restaurant hearing explosions. They may be streets away but the shock waves resonate through our homes and communities (Researcher in Iraq, December 2010).

Commitment to stay with the project is re-affirmed through the serious engagement with the struggles and political circumstances of the different research teams as they attempt to situate themselves both in the modern global context of Higher Education and the well-defined expectations of CARA which is helping to fund them. To uphold the critical importance of placing Iraqi voices at the heart of the

IRFP, and to build new communities of knowledge and academic practice requires all of us, including those academics ensconced in the safety of the West, to try to re-imagine research for the rebuilding of Iraq. The accounts of IRFP scholars, whose projects were selected for funding according to criteria focused on potential, reflects the IRFPs underlying capacity building goals and begin to exemplify just what is involved here.

REFERENCES

Adriaensens, D. (2011). *Further destruction of Iraq's Higher Education: Blazing fires, forged degrees and silencer guns,* Brussells Tribunal Executive Committee (01 December 2011) http://www .brussellstribunal.org/pdf/HigherEducation011211.pdf(accessed 6 December2011).

Baker, R., Ismael, S. T., & Ismael, T. Y. (2009*) Cultural Cleansing in Iraq Why Museums Were Looted, Libraries Burned and Academics Murdered.* London: Pluto Press.

Clough, P. (2010) *Narratives and Fictions in Educational Research* , Buckingham:

Open University Press

Fuller &Adriaensens (2009).'Wiping the Slate Clean'. In Baker, R. W., Ismael, S. T., & Ismael, T. V. (Eds.), *Cultural Cleansing in Iraq: Why Museums Were Looted, Libraries Burned, and Academics Murdered.* London: Pluto Press.

Lavia, J., & Moore, M. (2010).*Decolonizing Community Contexts: Cross-Cultural Perspectives on Policy and Practice.* London: Routledge.

Marfleet, P., & Chatty, D. 'Iraq's refugees – beyond 'tolerance', *RSC Forced Migration Policy Brief no. 4.* (Oxford: Refugees Studies Centre at the University of Oxford, 2003).

Moore, M. (Ed) (2000), *Insider Perspectives on Inclusion: raising voices, raising issues.* Sheffield: Philip Armstrong.

Nature Editorial (2010). Support refugee scientists, *Nature,* 4 November, Volume *468*, 5. Macmillan Publishers Limited.

Rowlatt, B, &Witwit, M. (2010) *Talking About Jane Austen in Baghdad: the true story of an unlikely friendship.* London: Penguin Books.

Seabrook, J. (2009) *The Refuge and the Fortress: Britain and the Flight from Tyranny.* Palgrave Macmillan.

Szenasi, J. (2010) 'I am a certain person when I am here, it is not who I am': Refugees Voices within communities of change, In J. Lavia and M. Moore (Eds.), *Decolonizing Community Contexts: Cross-Cultural Perspectives on Policy and Practice.* London: Routledge.

Tuhiwai Smith, L. (2002) (5th impression) *Decolonizing Methodologies: Research and Indigenous People.* London: Zed Books.

MOHANAD AHMED, HASSAN, SUHAD AHMED, ALI AL-ZAAG
AND MICHAEL R BARER

1. PROGRESS THROUGH OVERCOMING OBSTACLES IN TUBERCULOSIS RESEARCH: A SYNERGY BETWEEN DEVELOPING THE ACADEMY AND HEALTHCARE

'Making Tomorrow Better than Today'

INTRODUCTION

Our project originated in the minds of two Iraqi academics. One provided a spark for the CARA Iraq programme, the other saw how development of tuberculosis (TB) research could serve both regeneration of the academy and the Iraqi community. In engaging with the programme we discovered common motivations and aspirations. We planned many activities that succeeded and many that failed. Our work required many sacrifices and encountered difficult attitudes amongst colleagues and within institutions. Finally we are confronted by how to make our progress permanent.

BACKGROUND

Although the problem of tuberculosis is well recognized and methods for diagnosis based on direct observation of cough samples and lab cultivation of the organism have been established for many years, the organism is dangerous and handling of live cultures requires demanding biosafety measures (e.g., Boehme, et al, 2007). Our project started with an appreciation that the problem of TB is not well described in Iraq and that modern methods based on detecting the TB bacillus' DNA without growing the organism could remove the need for expensive facilities. So the work grew from the experience of our two Iraq microbiologists in molecular DNA studies and the opportunity to apply this to an important disease.

While thinking these points through Mohanad went to a biotechnology meeting in Turkey where he happened to see a stall promoting molecular TB diagnostic kits. Mohanad recalled a prior discussion with his wife Suhad, in which he had proposed that some of the family's money should be reserved to purchase scientific materials. Why should she accept this? Why should the family's capacity to build a house or buy a car be reduced to support his career? In the final analysis Suhad is also a committed scientist and was persuaded that this investment would be in the

H. Brunskell-Evans & M. Moore (Eds.), Reimagining Research for Reclaiming the Academy in Iraq: Identities and Participation in Post-Conflict Enquiry: The Iraq Research Fellowship Programme, 17–24.
© 2012 Sense Publishers. All rights reserved.

interest of their careers and the wellbeing of the family. Mohanad subsequently purchased TB molecular diagnostic kits and returned to Iraq, still with his plans relatively unformed.

Mohanad had seen an important career opportunity in TB because there was no current research in this field in Kerbala, a city that receives annually more than twenty million pilgrims to the shrine of Imam Hussein, the grandson of the prophet Mohamed. This situation raises interest in the degree to which the problem of TB in this city originated from within its own population or from the travellers. A discussion with Dr Hassan about the clinical situation for TB diagnosis and management in the city reinforced enthusiasm for the project and the spark from CARA was turned into the candle of the first application.

So now the project needed to make its English connections and, with the minor detail of successfully competing amongst more than 30 other applications, a UK participant was sought. Out of the blue, Mike received an email suggesting his involvement with an Iraqi and an organization he had never heard of. Why should he participate? Could the notion that the project offered limited scientific value and feasibility be balanced against Mike's commitment to global development and sense of responsibility towards the Iraqi nation following the invasion? Ultimately, despite an equivocal initial assessment of the proposal, he was impressed by the thoughtfulness and originality of the Mohanad's draft document. When in due course he learned the background to CARA, its history and its aims, his commitment was secured.

CARA arranged for Mohanad to visit Leicester to discuss the project. From his experience in working in Bangladesh, Ethiopia and the Gambia, Mike was concerned that, while the basic molecular principle proposed was sound, the specific method required reliable and sophisticated equipment that might be challenging for successful application in Kerbala. He thought that a different method of DNA analysis should be used and was nervous that Mohanad would feel insulted that his proposal might be altered. In the event, the meeting in Leicester was a triumphant exchange in which Mohanad's eagerness to learn and gain new experience was mixed with Mike's need to appreciate the realities of working in Kerbala and we approached the first workshop with optimism.

PLANNING

Our first plenary meeting was a mixture of excitement, bewilderment and frustration. In the beginning we were at a loss to think why should we listen to the apparent ramblings of social scientists who we assumed would know nothing of the rigors involved in scientific proof? Through the mists of confusion there emerged the beginnings of recognition that we had common problems and a respect for our very different disciplines. The IRFP participants faced the need to focus on achievable objectives that could be recognized by all research teams.

While all parties appreciated the opportunity provided by the CARA and its IFRP programme there was concern that plenary sessions and a 'one size fits all' approach to developing project plans could impose a pattern of progress that was retardant for the TB group and too fast for others. It was a challenge to complete the first planning phase in this context but also fascinating and pleasurable to hear about areas of research quite alien to biomedical scientists. Possibly as a consequence of this, within our group we felt a genuine personal warmth and sense of common purpose. Against this backdrop, our plan was produced to address four principle research questions:

- Would application of our chosen molecular analytical technique, known by the acronym LAMP, to standard coughed up (sputum) samples improve detection of TB cases over the standard microscopy-based analysis?
- Would this comparison (LAMP vs. microscopy) be affected in patients who had recently received antibiotics (these are widely available without prescription)?
- What was the frequency of resistance to rifampicin, a key antibiotic for TB treatment and was this related to prior use of antibiotics for other conditions?
- Most human TB is transmitted from person to person but some comes from cattle. Could we determine the balance between human- and cattle-derived TB in Kerbala?

All of this fell within jointly recognised motives to relieve the stigma of TB for patients and doctors alike and to create a positive progressive atmosphere. In this context patients often refuse diagnostic tests and hide their conditions. Doctors working at TB centres may have certain issues. For example, they may feel they have been sent there as a punishment for being perceived as trouble makers. Our aspiration was to counter these attitudes and raise awareness of TB.

It is not our purpose to report on our findings here but our experiences should be set against the nature of our task. The first IRFP workshop broke up in good spirits and the UK team returned to a frozen Christmas the Iraqis to their routine daily perils and frustrations. Something more than a plan to deliver some prosaic TB research had been achieved; the experience had opened the door for many of us to re-examine the arts/science alleged dichotomy in academia.

PROCESS

Over the next few months Mohanad was charged with setting up the collection of samples, establishing his laboratory base and engaging both co-workers and collaborators. Though sensitive to the constraints expressed by Mohanad and Hassan, our plans had been developed along the lines of a UK based project where three years would be a standard cycle; it soon emerged from Mohanad that even to sustain an operational plan that could last three months would be a major achievement.

Much of the work involved collection and storage of samples and reagents by Mohanad. There were numerous physical, organisational and attitudinal obstacles:

In travelling Mohanad frequently faced roadblocks and delays so that his meetings or collections were missed. Once he was locked into a TB centre processing samples at night because his schedule was so disrupted. He is now adept at talking to security guards to extract himself.

The seasons are an issue for TB researchers in Iraq: 'when I was processing my samples in summer the temperature inside my lab was above 50 degrees and for safety reasons it is not possible to switch on air con even if there is electricity ... every 30 minutes I was suffocating and having to take off my personal protective clothing and gloves and breathe and then go back into the laboratory'. Electricity supplies are unreliable: 'we have two supplies in Kerbala, regular and emergency ... it was decided the university did not need emergency supply so they cut it and we must rely on generators... this means no lab technique that requires more than a few hours elect supply can be viable'. Provision of generators is no doubt a major undertaking; they are easily installed but equally, either the generator or its fuel are easily stolen unless continuously attended. Mohanad's lab cannot afford this.

'Then they constructed a new road near the university and cut the whole supply of electricity ...then there was a conflict between the university and the electricity supplier which went on for 4 months so we had NO electricity ... I had to store my samples then in the college of science where they had some electricity'. Sometimes samples had to be stored overnight in Mohanad's home. 'We were researching TB in the kitchen ...we had to think about what happens to the children ... we had to get the samples out either when they were sleeping or before they came back from nursery.'

ORGANISATION AND ATTITUDES

We met with many organisational and bureaucratic obstacles as the project went on. Suddenly, for instance, Mohanad would be required to find an essential collaborator 'I need official confirmation from the minister of health'– he phoned supporting the research. 'I need a letter from the minister of health'– a letter was sent supporting the research. 'I need permission from the coalition forces!'– this was offered as a possibility. And then, 'don't worry about that but now I want a letter from the minister of health establishing an official research team'– this was established! HOORAY!!!

We planned to collect samples every other day but through a confusion of professional relationships it was found to be impossible and many valuable samples were thrown away in a way which was disastrous for the project. Mohanad describes how 'the first agreement between me and the Centre was to collect samples on different days ... but then I found they only stored negative samples because they were afraid to store positive samples but they did not tell me because they thought I had connections and would make trouble so they got rid of the positive samples and gave me only positive samples from days I was there – they would not store any. When I went through the records I found positive cases but no samples ... I did not want to make it embarrassing or difficult for them so I had to go every day to collect samples and I had to go early and stay late so that they would not burn the samples.'

Life within his own institution was not easy: 'I hope I am encouraging my colleagues as they see the efforts I make but there is also jealousy and bad feeling

...structural and attitudinal difficulties ... people think I am doing something private for personal ambition and gain ... even in the meeting amongst Deans of the College and the President of a senior colleague criticized my stay in the UK ... saying TB had disappeared from Iraq 2,000 years ago ... my Dean said he was proud of me but it is a difficult situation ...'

Some people say that Mohammed has been affected by his trips to 'the outside', 'even contaminated, and we cannot take seriously the changes he proposes.' These objectors, Mohanad feels 'do not want to change ... they do not want tomorrow to be different from today'. Others who Mohammed tells about the research think his work is for his personal interest and gain and insist that there is no wider benefit. They tell him they do not want him to 'build his research on their shoulders'.

In spite of these difficulties Mohanad collected a valuable initial set of samples, which, in view of the practical difficulties in Kerbala, he brought to Leicester for processing. The initial results indicated a significant excess of LAMP positive over microscopy positive results. On his return he focussed on further collections and on surmounting the obstacles to establishing LAMP in his own lab. However, he faced many new challenges as his work and his results became more widely known.

TRIUMPHS, JEALOUSIES AND DISASTERS

As with any research that impinges on clinical practice there is an imperative to consider what should be done in response when results indicate that improvements in patient care could potentially be deployed. When Mohanad reported our results to the second CARA funded IFRP workshop the opportunity arose to discuss them with the regional World Health Organisation office. Our work was received with genuine interest and various suggestions were made regarding further studies and the way in which our research might support the clinical services. This is a major challenge and just how research can be pursued in this context to build capacity in the academy and enhance healthcare at the same time.

A simple interpretation of our results was that a significant number of cases of TB were being missed by the routine diagnostic services and that LAMP might be used more widely to support the TB service. However, there are many levels at which the consequences of tests influencing clinical care must be considered especially where the local infrastructure faces the kind of challenges prevalent in Iraq. Moreover, in many cases of TB the diagnosis is made clinically (without lab tests) so some of the patients with negative microscopy and positive LAMP had received treatment. Thus it was important to emphasise that the primary purpose of our work was academic and capacity building for the academy as opposed to work aimed at improving clinical service.

As is the case in the UK, no matter how many times these cautions are explained, many will apply simplistic interpretations, see unrealistic opportunities and attribute sinister motives to results of this sort. However, unlike the UK and for obvious reasons, the basic infrastructure in Iraq is less robust and has less regulatory counterbalances. Thus Mohanad had many more new challenges to contend with.

He gave numerous talks about the research project in Kerbala and at other centres. On one occasion colleagues from outside turned on a Kerbala physician and asked in an accusatory tone 'why don't you treat these people? 'Colleagues developed unrealistic expectations that Mohanad would include them in his publications and presented arguments such as 'I have the same specialty as Dr Hassan!' Another attitude was that his time and molecular analyses might be available to physicians for any target they selected.

Of course there were also suspicions and jealousies. Some colleagues asked why a foreign charity would wish to donate to Iraq. Why are they not supporting their own people and why is Mohanad's work being supported? Is there some hidden purpose here? These are not easy questions to answer in a cultural context that is so different from the UK.

And there were disasters. 'Once I found the labelling of my samples was not very clear ... the markers were water resistant but not alcohol resistant ... my wife will tell you, I was about to cry; I felt each sample was a fortune for me and they were lost.' Much later there was a catastrophe. Several hundred samples brought to Leicester were rendered useless by a change in processing and storage that, unknown to us, profoundly undermined the LAMP technique. 'we were very, very upset ... so much effort had gone into the collection.'

THE MEDIA AND ASSASSINATION OF ACADEMICS

Then of course there was the question of the media. Mohanad has found himself regularly invited to speak to reporters from within and outside Iraq about his work. But he faces threats of assassination if he takes part in public discussions of this sort. This is part of the background of academic life in Iraq. It appears that academics, who presumably can be seen as authoritative sources, are particularly targeted in this regard. This may simply reflect that, as a group potentially in the public eye, they are not security protected and are therefore easy targets. Mohanad has so far refused to be interviewed partly for this reason and partly because of his he understanding of the political context. He believes that if a scholar is assassinated it is significant in terms of reactions from other countries. However, politicians do not care about the individuals assassinated; rather they are concerned with projecting particular images globally. For example if Mohanad revealed to a reporter that there were difficulties with pursuing research he knows that his words would be quickly hijacked for propaganda purposes. 'The issue of assassination of academics and doctors has been with us for years to create fear so that people would be silent ... the real message was 'keep quiet and shut up' and this message is now perpetuated by those who have political power ... they think that academics and highly educated people are a threat to their authority.'

Analogies could be drawn between this experience and the environment in the UK relating to animal experimentation. Although the moral issues are quite different and the threat of a different order, there has been for some quarter of century a silencing of academics variously by individual choice, by pressure from colleagues and by some institutions. The situation has changed substantially in the last five years with a combination of a tough policing approach to animal campaigners who perpetrate or threaten violence (there have been car, nail and fire bombs in the UK) and individuals and groups who are prepared to be publically recognised as animal researchers. Mike had contemporaneous experience of this in his own institution where he has been interviewed about their new animal research building. No one else involved in the journalist's visit was prepared to be named so anxiety is still prevalent. Subsequently Leicester has been publicly praised for its open policy to the debate on animal research. 'At some level academics have to stand up for what they do'. Mike takes this view but recognises that the security situation would have to be transformed before this could apply in Iraq.

CONCLUDING REMARKS

Through all these trials, a body of robust research has been achieved and now needs to be reported. But has the primary purpose of the project been achieved and will there be a sustainable effect? As is so often the case, the final delivery of the research outcome will now take place after the resources and allocated time for the project have passed. Nonetheless, we can comment on what has emerged so far from the process. Out of necessity Mohanad has emerged with diplomatic skills he never thought would be his 'remember I grew up in a village ...we are the leaders of the tribe ... to resolve difficulties in the community we have to say things frankly, not seeking diplomacy ... this has created many problems for me in my life ... when I lived in Baghdad I needed to say things in a very diplomatic way and not rush through problems with people ... and now, in this project, I have had the opportunity to engage with people who have great skills for open and diplomatic communication and I am learning new things and new dimensions for my future through these engagements ... from Hasan and Mike I learned different ways of communication ... usually I tell what I feel nakedly ... I just tell it ...but they have taught me to say things with strength but less provocatively.' He has learnt that problems faced in delivering our work have to be discussed with great care. Simply to complain about obstacles, no matter how ludicrous, can be counterproductive. In particular, it is often security considerations that mean the work promised cannot come to fruition. Sensitivities in all areas are such that criticisms can rebound and the only way though is to make cooperation seem inviting and to deal with disasters in a blame free manner.

Suhad commented on sustainability saying 'I think the legacy of our IRFP involvement will be sustained. We will have postgraduate students and MSc students focusing on a TB programme and TB research. We will keep on working to establish a system for quality for research within the college is important as is accreditation of quality assurance. We must work to develop an exciting science curriculum, there is a great deal more to be done.' But she wonders, 'how can we create something sustainable when the environment is so out of control?' Strength accrued from participation in the IRFP can be discerned, 'the benefit of having someone doing research and publishing research in high impact journals cannot be underestimated and good practice cascades. For example, my dean became interested and asked me to convene a Round Table Discussion – but most lecturers in Iraq are tasked with being descriptive only, teaching without research and there is no culture of research-led teaching'. The excitement of the research journey is sometimes stifled by thoughts of the distance to be travelled and at one point of writing this chapter Mohanad looked up to reflect 'we are so far behind in microbiology in Iraq that if I study day and night I can't bridge the gap alone ... I feel like a researcher in infancy ... like a child, I need a good father, I need to take everything from you [Professor Barer]. I think what I want to learn is everything, the A-Z of your research career and life'. Mike replied 'well it's better if you have A-F maybe but then create your own F-Z of research and life – and you will do it much better than I'.

REFERENCE

Boehme, C. C., Nabeta, P., Henostroza, G., Raqib, R., Rahim, Z., Gerhardt, M., Sanga, E., Hoelscher, M., Notomi, T., Hase, T., Perkins, M. D. (2007). Operational feasibility of using loop-mediated isothermal amplification for diagnosis of pulmonary tuberculosis in microscopy centers of developing countries. *Journal of Clinical Microbiology, 45*(6), 1936–1940.

AMIR AL-AZRAKI, NADIA SEKRAN, MICHAEL POMERANTZ,
AND BRUCE WOODING

2. BANKING COLLAPSES: TRANSFORMING THE LEARNING ENVIRONMENT IN IRAQ THROUGH FORUM THEATRE

INTRODUCTION

This is the story of an experimental attempt, by a group of academics in Iraq, the UK and Canada, to introduce the practice known as 'Forum Theatre' into the Arts Faculty of the University of Basra and to study its reception and impact. We call the project 'Transforming the Learning Environment through Theatre' or TLET. Forum theatre is a practice invented and pioneered by the Brazilian director and teacher, Augusto Boal, in the 1970s, Forum Theatre invites spectators to alter and complete scenarios, presented by actors, which depict unsatisfactory personal and social situations in the spectators' own community. In his early work with the poor inhabitants of the barrios on the outskirts of Lima, Peru, he dubbed the practice 'rehearsals for the revolution.' More generally, the practice of trying out solutions to perceived problems by performing them can be seen as the rehearsal of all kinds of constructive possibilities in the participant's situation. Introducing the practice into a community previously unfamiliar with it entails considerable trial and error, as actors have to be trained to devise suitable scenarios for performance, while spectators have to be encouraged to engage with the process in an open and risk-taking way. Each new attempt to foster Forum Theatre in a community provides a fresh opportunity to study the particular challenges to be encountered and the relative successes and failures of the undertaking.

The IRFP TLET project bought together a range of academics from several countries and allowed for clear knowledge exchange. In particular, as the group's IFRP work forged new synergies, a relationship between the UK Central School of Speech and Drama and the University of Basra was forged enabling successful bidding for additional DelpHE monies. A generous further grant allowed for a 12 month project that set out to explore how drama can be used across the curriculum in lecture delivery from a broad range of faculty from the arts to agriculture to Islamic Banking. This work also includes an Iraq wide conference to be held at the University of Basra which will allow for further dissemination of both IRFP and DelpHE funded aspects of the group's work projects across the Higher Education system in Iraq.

H. Brunskell-Evans & M. Moore (Eds.), Reimagining Research for Reclaiming the Academy in Iraq:
Identities and Participation in Post-Conflict Enquiry: The Iraq Research Fellowship Programme, 25–37.

THE BEGINNING: SETTING THE CONTEXT

Funded by the Iraqi government and with the explicit expectation of contributing positively to the educational environment at home, Amir Al-Azraki arrived in Canada in 2007 to embark on a PhD in Theatre Studies at York University in Toronto. Up until this point he had been supported by CARA since 2006 and awarded Hardship Funding. In Canada he was immediately struck by the enabling of critical thinking and experiential learning within the Canadian Higher Education system. Complementing what he experienced in lectures and seminars was his encounter with Paulo Freire's ground-breaking book, *The Pedagogy of the Oppressed*. This was the first book he read in Canada and it spiralled his thinking into considering 'What if?' Might it be possible to change the 'relational dance' between students and academics in Iraqi universities to promote a dialogue in which knowledge is collaboratively constructed rather than unilaterally delivered? Having been nurtured in Iraqi educational institutions, Amir realised that Freire's postulation (quoted below) resonated quite strikingly with the learning environment in Iraqi universities as he had experienced it:

Education thus becomes an act of depositing, in which the students are the depositories and the teacher is the depositor. Instead of communicating, the teacher issues communiqués and makes deposits which the students patiently receive, memorize, and repeat. This is the 'banking' concept of education, in which the scope of action allowed to the students extends only as far as receiving, filing, and storing the deposits. They do, it is true, have the opportunity to become collectors or cataloguers of the things they store. But in the last analysis, it is the people themselves who are filed away through the lack of creativity, transformation, and knowledge in this (at best) misguided system (The Pedagogy of the Oppressed p 72).

Freire remained an inspiring figure in Amir's thinking, but it was not until encountering Augusto Boal, another South American, that a relevant practical and theatrical application was discovered. From an urgent need to utilise Boal's Forum Theatre as a contribution to the rebuilding of Iraqi Higher Education, the seed of the idea of Forum Theatre practice located in the theatre department in the University of Basra was born.

The original idea, subsequently much modified, was to document and evaluate the establishment within the English Department of the University of Basra of an English-language theatre group dedicated to fostering academic community, developing students' skills in the English language and teachers' communicative pedagogy, and enlarging their understanding of modern and contemporary English theatre.

The proposal was presented to CARA to be considered for funding as part of the Iraq Research Fellowship Programme, but CARA requested that the proposal be revised to fit more precisely the aim of the fellowship, which is to enhance teaching capacities and develop regional and Iraqi research collaboration. After being modified, the proposal was tentatively approved and a research group established, consisting initially (in addition to Amir himself as author of the original proposal) of Robert Fothergill, Professor Emeritus of Theatre at York University as a Principal Investigator (PI), Bruce Wooding, Head of the School of

Professional and Community Development at the Central School of Speech and Drama, University of London, as co-PI, and Abdul Kareem Abood, Professor in the Theatre Department at the Fine Arts College, University of Basra, as Director of the Project. The University of Basra, founded in 1964, is situated in the city of Basra, Iraq. In the present day the University consists of fourteen colleges located on three campuses around the city of Basra, along with research facilities and dormitories. The other partners were York University and Central School of Speech and Drama. As the work progressed, two other members were recruited to the group. They were Dr. Alia Badr (researcher) and Nadia Sekran (researcher and writer). As the work progressed, two other members were recruited to the group. They were Dr. Alia Badr (researcher) and Nadia Sekran (researcher and writer).

The initial group (Robert, Amir, Bruce, and Kareem) met at the second IFRP Induction Workshop in Amman in April, 2010, to finalise their proposal. After intensive sessions and discussions, the proposal was modified again with the title 'Transforming the Learning Environment through Theatre: Basra University as a Model', referred to henceforth as TLET. In addition to changing the medium of the project from English into Arabic, the project shifted its attention from students of English to the problems in the learning environment at the University of Basra. This decision was made so students could work in their mother tongue to access, for example, political and psychological expression that might well have been hampered and difficult to explore using a foreign language medium.

The vision of TLET became one of a research project designed to explore the ways in which interactive theatre can contribute to the transformation of the teaching-learning environment in an Iraqi university. It started from the assumption that some aspects of the learning environment at Basra University were relatively dysfunctional, constituting barriers and disincentives to productive interaction among teachers and students. Authoritarian teaching styles, unbalanced power relations between students and teachers, widespread cheating in exams and problems of gender relations were among the focal issues to be tackled. The project sought to test the effectiveness of the kind of theatrical practice and pedagogical method pioneered by Augusto Boal in modifying awareness and behaviour. The implementation of the process, and its impact and effectiveness, were to be the objects of a series of research investigations, with the results to be disseminated in the literature on Applied Theatre and shared with other Iraqi universities for possible adoption.

In fact, the use of theatre for social awareness and social change has been introduced in many developing countries. To cite a few examples in Bangladesh the Danish embassy introduced theatre and drama as a communication and empowerment tool within the fisheries sub-sector programme of the Agricultural Sector Programme (ASP), in the Water Supply and Sanitation programme (WSSP) and in the Human Rights and Good Governance Programme (HRGG). In Tanzania, advocated by Shrosbree and Hamblett, theatre was used to explore the reasons that prevent people from participating in the electoral process. Also, community theatre in Eretria was utilized to deal with such issues as AIDS, reconciliation and the education of women. More specifically, Boal's Forum Theatre has been used in

27

many countries all over the world to deal with a variety of issues and problems. For example, in Canada, Mixed Company Theatre, led by its director Simon Malbogat, who is considered a pioneer of Forum Theatre, has been using it in Ontario schools to address issues of, for instance, bullying, drugs, racism, alcohol, and violence. And in Syria, Mary al-Yas has introduced an experiment in the use of interactive theatre in the public schools to address issues related to children's psychological and social problems.

CONTEXT – POLITICS, GENDER, ETHICS, RISKS

The political situation in Basra is replete with tensions and conflicts, and it seems that political and religious parties are able to exert a powerful control on the environment of the University. In fact, several attempts to expel the College of Fine Arts from the University have been conducted by certain religious figures, on the pretext that work in the Fine Arts contravenes Islamic teachings. In such a risky situation where interference, usually with violence, by religious parties and militias into the affairs of the students' community has been a noticeable issue, the Forum Theatre project had to be undertaken with caution.

Gender represents a critical issue in the University of Basra. Such an issue can be seen through a number of lenses within this context. One of these is discrimination. For instance, in many cases female academics find a problem in incorporating themselves in situations where they believe they have a right to be involved. At work, female academics are not given status according to their scientific qualifications and experience, but have been excluded from opportunities from which they can benefit just as much as male academics, including nominations for positions or scholarships. Sweeping judgments and generalizations are also another part of the problem. Female academics are treated and judged according to the generally unfair views that society traditionally has about them as women. This unfortunately may also be true of another lower-status subgroup like female students in the University. In class, they often face situations where they are discouraged from participating because of shyness, embarrassment, and fear of being criticized by male peers. They also encounter difficulties in communicating with male teachers, especially those who are biased towards their own gender.

Our work has not set out to offend any group, but aims essentially to encourage free speech across all peoples regardless of their affiliation by focusing on social issues. We have attempted to avoid political and religious issues written across party lines. To avoid any criticism of being a post-colonial project, the researchers introduced the project as something to be taken into ownership by Iraqi scholars. We did not set out to be purist Forum practitioners, didactically following Boal's writings exercise by exercise, but practitioners who were trained to be attuned to cultural and individual needs, and who would select from the work those aspects that would create relevant interventions and discussions within the immediate context.

We adopted the Ethics Guidelines employed at CSSD in London, and passed our proposal and ethics paper through their Ethics committee which accepted it.

There was no such committee in the University of Basra and so, by using a UK-based university for the process, we enabled the work to have currency in the international market.

In the meetings in Amman we gave considerable time to the discussion of risk. A key concern was the safety of students, and indeed staff, who would be participating. If we were to explore politicized issued at the local level of the university, or more broadly on a national level, were any areas to be regarded as taboo? What would happen if an audience member challenged the actors to play in an inappropriate or politically dangerous way? Would female students be more exposed to such risk than males?

These issues were very real and vital to discuss and reflect upon. However, as the work developed, more practical risks emerged and these had to be managed too. By the time we applied for a grant under the DelPHE scheme – Development Partnerships in Higher Education, operated by the British Council – we had a broader idea of the risks that we would have to consider in the life of the CARA funded work.

Among a number that were considered, some in particular were assessed in terms of the likelihood of their occurring and their potential impact on the project. Regarded as relatively unlikely, but of potentially high impact were: a shortfall of suitable student participants; difficulty in recruiting in appropriate academics; and improper management of financial resources. The first two could be met by the recruitment of MA students if necessary, and by encouragement from the University leadership; the third would require strict and open financial scrutiny. Another risk, regarded as quite high and a potential obstacle to success, was the possibility that female academics might encounter difficulty in leaving Iraq. To deal with this possibility, meetings should be arranged for Jordan, Lebanon or Turkey, and as a last resort, meetings might have to be conducted via Skype. Highly problematic, but considered unlikely, was the risk of losing the support of the Principals of either or both of CSSD and the University of Basra. Finally, and perhaps most worrying, was the possibility of a serious backlash against the participants, or at least serious resistance to the whole thrust of the project. It was agreed that, to meet this risk, continuous monitoring of the environment should be maintained, along with clearly expressed institutional support. As a further mitigation it was suggested that the TLET group might have to work in a less public arena, and that a list of 'taboo' topics should be drawn up. The development of clear risk assessments aided project management and gave a clear focus and direction to the work.

CHRONOLOGY: MEETINGS, TRAINING, REHEARSALS, PERFORMANCES

As already noted, the core research group met first in Amman in April 2010 to frame and develop the proposal. In September 2010 some of the group met again in Amman to attempt to refine and focus the research methodology and to set up a time-scale for operation and delivery.

Training occurred across the project. A summer course, focused on Boal's teaching, was held at CSSD and attended by members of the core research team, including Kareem and Amir, and joined by Michael Pomerantz who was now incorporated into the group. Michael is a retired senior educational psychologist, University of Sheffield trainer and consultant who was recruited to help develop the team into a Research Community. The course consisted of warm-up exercises each morning chosen from 'Games for Actors and Non-actor' and chosen from the specific sensory areas Boal focussed on to encourage trust and confidence in his 'spect-actors'– his term for spectators who become participants. The course continued by chronologically moving through all the stages Boal went through to finally arrive at Forum Theatre. Using one approach a scene/play was created by two groups to use as a Forum piece. The role of the 'Joker' (Facilitator or director) was examined through exercises, demonstration and discussion. Then the participants presented the Forum, using the other group as the spect-actors (audience).The process stopped and started when people struggled with the Joker role and gave suggestions – as this was a course in understanding the techniques rather than delivering a full production.

Also in London, and at the prompting of Michael Pomerantz, the team decided that we should form an innovative and interdisciplinary Research Community (or RC) to facilitate the production of anticipated and evidence based learning outcomes with measurable impact. This was to be established within an amicable and non-hierarchical learning environment and international host culture. This group was carefully designed to foster and support close team building, safe practice, shared values, effective communication patterns, equitable and practical workload allocation and task and project deadlines.

We wanted to create a working Forum that would allow a professional debate about both the research questions (RQs) and the research methodology (RM). We wanted to build a space to learn from one another and to move out of isolated silos of day-to-day practice. In essence, we wanted to explore the impact of Forum Theatre (FT) training, rehearsals and performances at the University of Basra. Our hope was that FT would eventually be seen in Iraq as a helpful way to promote knowledge construction and social justice. It could ideally be seen as a rather special way to address social issues like bullying, teasing, marginalisation, cheating, authoritarian practices and gendered interactions. It might increase the repertoire of participants and demonstrate assertion and more socially appropriate behaviours in tense situations. It would privilege the voices of those less often heard.

Here are the initial TLET Research Community values that were tentatively agreed in London for our work together. This list was unfinished and in draft form:

- We support Forum Theatre and Augusto Boal's work.
- We support knowledge construction as a shared teacher/student activity as opposed to an over-reliance on a purely knowledge-dissemination pedagogy.
- We support social justice, emancipation, fair play and inclusion.
- We support a host culture where participation is highly valued and RC members are not punished for 'getting it wrong' in Forum Theatre sessions.

- We support an Iraqi interpretation of Forum Theatre so this work is set in a cultural context.
- We support teambuilding, audience participation and experiential teaching approaches that are safe and have boundaries.
- We support working within an ethical framework where all participants know their rights and responsibilities.
- We support work in the Arabic language.
- We support the transfer of Forum Theatre to other departments and other universities.
- We support research to build upon and expand the Forum Theatre experience.

After the August 2010 visit to London, the Iraqi academics took their learning back to Basra and undertook to disseminate it to other colleagues and to the students who were being recruited as the actors. Back in Toronto, Amir met with Simon Malbogat and participated in his Mixed Company Theatre summer school in September 2009, while Bruce Wooding visited Sango Ganguly, director of Jana Sanskriti, a leading exponent of Forum Theatre in Kolkata, India. Both members were attempting to deepen their knowledge of the practice. In December 2010 Amir returned to Basra University to provide further training for all participants there. A model of international knowledge exchange and a network of practice were being established over the life of the project.

GETTING DOWN TO BUSINESS

The impact of implementing FT techniques within the university setting of Basra has been looked upon from three perspectives. The first concerns the researchers themselves; the second relates to the trainee performers; and the third has to do with the audience as 'spect-actors'. Thus, the data specific to this research evolved from three main sources: the researchers, the trainees and the audience. The trainees' questionnaires and journals represent the first part of the data.

From the outset, a number of researchers from the College of Fine Arts were trained on how to perform a Forum show. Then, they took the responsibility of training students from the same college. Ten students were selected to participate in the project as FT performers. However, three of them quit for different reasons. One of these reasons was that female students among those who quit could not persuade their families to allow them keep participating in the project as they thought that the work carried risks. Therefore, seven students remained to witness the rehearsals.

Throughout the rehearsals, the trainees were asked to report their own comments and remarks on the whole process by documenting them in journals which were completed early in the day of each rehearsal, reflecting their real involvement in the project. At the same time, the trainers themselves recorded reflections on the trainees, by observing the levels of development in their skills in enacting a piece of FT in theatrical performances that were regarded to a large extent as new in form and content, not only for them but also for the audience.

The questionnaires the trainees took included a pre-questionnaire administered to those involved before getting trained on practising FT, and a post-questionnaire given at the end of the rehearsals. Further, they were given a number of open-ended research questions to answer. In forming these questions the researchers tried to get profoundly into the concerns and assumptions the trainee performers had concerning their participation in the project. It is also worth mentioning that the rehearsals as well as performances were video-recorded and photos were taken to further evidence the trainees' development levels of skills in performing FT shows that can motivate interaction among the audience. This is considered another source of data to be utilized in the analysis.

Two Forum performances were mounted in the Faculty of Fine Arts. While the first show took place on the stage of the Theatre Department, the second show was put on at the lab established with CARA funds, which is located in the Faculty of Fine Arts. Each show, with three perspectives rehearsed consecutively and with the spect-actors' interventions and discussions, lasted 45 minutes. The scripts were created collectively by the actors and the researchers, working in an improvisatory fashion. The main issue that the script tackled was how a teacher can be biased sometimes, being oppressive of male students while being lenient with female students, especially when cheating occurs in the classroom. The shows were realistically presented, and the spect-actors felt very familiar with the issue depicted. After the first show finished and spect-actors were asked to take part, a number of students and even teachers keenly responded in an attempt to fix the problem through replacing the actors on stage and through debate as well. Then, the researchers conducted surveys, interviews and questionnaires to study the impact of such a new theatre in the university.

The questionnaire that was administered to the audience (in Arabic) was divided into two parts. The first part included fifteen tick-off questions about their experience with FT – if they had any, the themes presented, challenges and fears related to their participation in the shows, and more significantly, questions about whether or not FT could contribute to transform the relationship between the teacher and the student within the university setting. The second part of the questionnaire contained five open-ended questions whose answers would illuminate the audience's reflections on what they had watched and perceived. These questions asked about the opinions the audience held about the shows themselves and their interaction and participation, including issues that surprised them about the show. It is worth mentioning that the principal aim behind constructing a questionnaire like this was to bring forth a possibility to change concepts traditionally adopted by an academic society whose members tend to accept and defend issues only because they are accustomed to believe in them, and reject any attempt to change or criticise. Hence, it was not easy to convince them to react positively to the whole process.

DATA COLLECTION AND ANALYSIS

Responses were collected from 63 attendees and analysed. One of the most profound findings highlighted a serious consequence of the research methodological decision not to interview attendees but to rely on a more traditional quantitative questionnaire e approach which is more customary in this social context. Some of our team members felt that this anonymous questionnaire survey would yield more objective and less personally intrusive data than might be gained from interview interviews or focus groups.

To a general question as to whether the introduction of Forum Theatre into this community could be seen as posing 'a risk', 7 attendees answered 'yes', 18 answered 'fairly', 35 answered 'no', and three provided no response. By aggregating the 7 who chose 'yes' with the 18 who said 'fairly', we see a total of 25 worrying indicators which represents almost 40% of the sample surveyed. While it may be reassuring to find that 35 of the 63 (56%) did not see potential risks associated with FT, we are left quite curious about why so many (25 or almost 40%) reported risk as an issue for them. Within interviews (which did not actually happen) we might have asked attendees to elaborate in greater detail on what they meant by their abbreviated responses on an anonymous questionnaire.

At this stage in our research we have not learned in-depth answers to questions like:

- How might FT pose a risk to you personally?
- What do you mean by risk?
- What precisely are the dangers?
- How might we take steps to reduce or remove this risk?
- How serious are the risks?
- Are you personally prepared to undertake these risks?
- Should FT only be targeted at some participants?
- Who might benefit best from FT?

While this disappointment associated with unasked questions is noted, it will hopefully inform further discussion within the FT research group. We now know from other CARA colleagues working on parallel Iraqi research projects to ours and also writing in this same book that some interviews are being used with emerging success as an alternative, recognized and quite legitimate way to do social science research in Iraq. We now have further hard evidence supporting the value of widening research methodology to embrace more qualitative approaches and to privilege insights obtained from a deeper exploration of the phenomena under investigation.

PRAGMATICS AND OPERATIONAL ISSUES

The pragmatic and organisational issues that arose during the project are worthy of note. Meeting in person and electronically was not always smooth. Face to face meetings took place in London and Jordan but these were interrupted by visa issues and the availability of team members. Getting to London was difficult for two Iraqi academics; they had to spend a lot of time waiting for a visa and this took up a larger than expected percentage of the budget. The sessions in Jordan also meant that for some project members it was difficult to get a visa and so access wasn't equal for all at all times. This is something to be aware of when organising similar future work.

When Bruce tried to visit Iraq it became complex, as we could not establish if the letter of invitation had arrived. Numerous phone calls were made to the Embassy in London. The phone was only picked up once and none of the messages we left were responded to. This was disappointing and meant further knowledge transfer to all participants in Basra was hampered. We note the complexity here in case researchers decide to do work across the two countries. We experienced visa and travel complexities in both countries!

Electronic communication, whilst useful and necessary, was not always easy. Some emails were too long and were not translated into Arabic, some emails read abruptly causing concern about control and colonial behaviour and Skype communication was not always easy to connect to and during sessions when discussing would cut off .We had to remain positive and flexible. We had to make the best of less than perfect moments and had to develop trust in each other to ensure communication. We had to rely on phone calls at times and often used mobiles. Again this is something to consider when planning a project – communication was not without cost.

Even money transfer was problematic and took longer than expected. This pushed the boundaries of trust with some team members. The finances remained a key topic of debate throughout the project as UK and Iraqi systems of financial accountability were not the same. For example, it was not always possible to meet requests for receipts. This is something for researchers to consider in risk assessment when doing such work. Another challenge was that of a bureaucratic nature. The hierarchical systems in both the UK and the Iraq occasionally did not help the smooth running of the project. Getting letters and institutional approval across two different operational timescales caused some tensions. Senior personnel needed convincing. We all had to learn to understand that sometimes decisions and actions could not move with the speed we desired.

The delay in money transfer led to a delay in the rebuild of the laboratory theatre and this impacted on the start date for the project. Whilst this did not impact in a highly adverse way it was far from ideal and did not help with the smooth initiation of the work in Iraq. The refurbishment of the room was key to the success of the project – it gave a spatial identity to the work and provided a pleasant environment in which to develop the new work. Dr. Kareem had the vision to create a comfortable and well equipped rehearsal room. He was passionate about creating a space where new work could be made and a place that would give a physical identity to the emerging work. He was able to convince the University authorities to give him a room to refurbish and we used money from the budget to make the lab come to fruition. As soon as we were able to organize the transfer of money by Western Union from London to Iraq, Dr Kareem busily set about getting in the work people and decorators. The space created had a positive impact on the work – there was somewhere safe and comfortable to work. Given the risky nature of the work and the concerns we had to create a safe environment this was an important part of the process. A space adjoined the laboratory theatre was created to encourage research. Dr Kareem's vision was to have a small library, computers with Internet access and comfortable office furniture so that both staff and students could access information. We encountered a problem here, as there was insufficient money to complete the work. The room was later equipped with resources from the DelpHE project moneys.

A further problem with the research aspect of the project occurred with accessing on-line journals. Not only could we not have the computer in the lab area but we could not get the academics access to on-line journals. We had hoped that, as with some other of the projects with other UK universities, the academics would be able to access on-line journal systems. However, the policy at CSSD prohibited anyone except for employees and registered students to have access. This was a blow that we had to ameliorate by posting on the CARA NING website and through the sharing of paper and other publications that the UK and Canadian academics had access to themselves.

OUTCOMES, OUTPUTS, IMPACT, CELEBRATION, RETURN TO ORIGINAL ASPIRATION

There were Many Positive Outcomes to Celebrate. As Participants Said:

I learnt the ability of raising the problem with no fear.

It leaves bad people with no masks and lets their intentions be known.

It changes the way of objective thinking towards the university environment.

Audience members also reflected such positive experiences:

I was surprised because it is a strange kind of theatre. I didn't expect such theatre to exist in Iraq but I believe it will create a noticeable change.

This is a democratic idea! A dialogue was created between the actors and the audience. The participation by and the acceptance of the audience to a new kind of theatre – I don't know why. Maybe the audience are thirsty for such kind of theatre.

I was impressed by the flexibility in this show and the ability to accept and listen to other opinion. This is what makes others think.

The work improves the mentality of the students and the teaching staff.

As academics the work gave us a strong foundation for the successful bid made to DelpHE. We were one of a small number of successful applicants and the only arts based project. The impact and enthusiasm from the key drivers of the work in Iraq led to a wider recruitment to look more broadly at drama education and its potential to develop active learning in a Higher Education setting. Fifty percent of academic participants recruited were women and there was a good mix of experienced and emerging scholars involved.

Prior to the CARA funded project the Theatre Department at Basra did not explore drama education and Forum Theatre. There is now a capacity to develop this work and one academic in particular is keen to develop a course for primary school teachers to open minds to the explorative and reflective power of practical drama.

As a team we have learnt from each other, shared knowledge and developed new knowledge. All of us have learnt about cross cultural work and the particular dynamics of a Canadian, UK and Iraqi triangle. We have all been enabled to have meaningful professional development and to do high-level knowledge transfer. We haven't always agreed, but the grit of the disagreements has led us to refine and clarify our work and to reconsider some of our assumptions about givens.

CONCLUSION

Having read the chapter, we hope readers will have enjoyed our journey and that they have encountered a model of pedagogy in an Iraqi Higher Education setting, as well as having gained insights into project planning and management cross-culturally, and further have encountered the debate regarding the quantitative and qualitative research methodology in arts in the Iraqi context. We have learnt a great deal through the project as researchers and how qualitative research is valuable and how Forum Theatre can be a very useful method to explore issues in a university setting. There is a space for such work and it has enormous potential.

The project contributes to the Iraqi academy in two ways. First, through its interactive shows, the project has deconstructed the problematic relationship between the teacher and the student; the responses of the spect-actors, who were either students or teachers, show that they have apprehended the oppressive and unbalanced nature of this relationship, which in turn affects negatively the learning environment and the communication process between the teacher and the student. Their realization has urged them to seek realistic solutions for the problems that have caused such an unhealthy learning atmosphere. Such a self-reflection on the relationship between the student and the teacher was for the first time explored publically and critically through Forum Theatre.

Second, there is scope to take the work further in Basra University. Staff outside of the theatre field were able to work in an interdisciplinary fashion and greatly increased their knowledge about Forum Theatre and gained in confidence in implementing the method. Practical knowledge that can be used in different learning contexts was enhanced. The project can be considered as a cornerstone that could motivate Iraqi educators to rethink the current adopted pedagogical approaches in the Iraqi universities. The results of the project will be looked at by the President of the University of Basra who hopefully will disseminate the newly gained knowledge to the policy makers and curriculum designers in the Ministry of

Higher Education, which we expect, can take a serious action to deal with the issues raised by our project.

Throughout the project we established that Forum can be a powerful tool in the Iraqi context. The first time Forum has occurred in a university setting in Iraq enabled a democratic process in which the participants involved their critical and free thinking. We believe this innovation has made a difference and provides a foundation for further development of transformative, critically engaged teaching and learning methodology. The evidence suggests the student audience felt they were heard. They had begun to be given voice.

Forum Theatre is a flexible, robust, inspirational tool. The performance travelled across the university to three different university departments and an interdisciplinary group encountered the work. Equally, the researchers were also from an interdisciplinary team and this kept in line with the aim of the CARA project to develop interdisciplinary discussions and knowledge transfer.

The Forum Theatre has added value to the University of Basra as it planted a seed for change and created a safe space for students and teachers to experiment and explore important issues related to teaching and learning in the university setting that might not be addressed in another place. The work initiated conversations that arguably would not have been happening and we believe it is beginning to impact on the pedagogy of Higher Education. This modest beginning has led to a re-examination of presenting, communicating and creating knowledge. We noted a shift to a focus on processes which were as important as the content in the project.

The journey was not without challenge. There was no utopia. Our ideals had to be transformed but we created an intergenerational research community across three different continents that embraced divergent thinking. We have been deeply inspired by our academic colleagues that took part in the Iraq Fellowship Programme along with the CARA leadership and care that enabled us to be part of a wider thriving international research community that had such a broad range of interests and met over a long period of time. We feel privileged to have taken part in this intercultural work. To travel, to meet, to discuss, to share knowledge and to learn about our various contexts has been a very special experience and a key by-product of the original proposal.

REFERENCES:

Boal, A. (2002).*Games for Actors and Non-actors* (2nd ed.). London: Routledge.
Freire, P. (2001). *The Pedagogy of the Oppressed* (30th ed.). London: Continuum International Publishing Group Ltd.

NADJE AL-ALI, HUDA AL-DUJAILI, INASS AL-ENEZY AND IRADA
AL-JEBOURY

3. WE DON'T DO NUMBERS! REIMAGINING GENDER AND SELVES

INTRODUCTION

We are a team of female Iraqi academics of different disciplinary, and generational backgrounds, based in different locations (Irada and Inass in Baghdad; Huda in Amman and Nadje, the half-Iraqi in London). We all have very different life experiences and relations to Iraq. Irada is both an academic in media studies but also an established writer; Huda is an economist; Inass a political scientist and Nadje, the PI of the team, is an anthropologist specializing in gender studies. All of us are also involved in women's rights and wider civil society activism. What brought us together is passion for our work and a commitment to bring about change for the better.

This chapter will reflect on the processes and experiences of us working together across our differences and similarities while also negotiating and engaging with Iraqi and international academics from both the social and natural sciences in the context of CARA's Iraqi Research Fellowship Programme (IRFP). We will address the challenges of introducing gender and qualitative research into Iraqi Higher Education. But we will also share the way the research process affected our sense of self and our worldviews. The chapter attempts to address the following questions: What does it mean to do qualitative research in a context of on-going insecurity, lawlessness and conflict? What does it involve to be able to carry out informal in depth interviews with female academics? How did the findings influence our perceptions about the role of female academics and Iraqi women more generally? And how did the research impinge on our own identities as female academics and as Iraqis?

Even if we do not want to fall into simplistic notions of before and after the invasion of 2003, there is no doubt that Iraqi women did not gain the rights and freedom promised to them in the run up to the US-led invasion. There has been a significant deterioration in women's labour force participation as well as in legal rights pertaining to marriage, divorce, inheritance and child custody (Al-Ali, 2007).General social norms and attitudes towards women have become more conservative and restrictive in recent years (ibid.). At the same time, there has been an institutionalization of gender-based discrimination in many contexts as well as

H. Brunskell-Evans & M. Moore (Eds.), Reimagining Research for Reclaiming the Academy in Iraq:
Identities and Participation in Post-Conflict Enquiry: The Iraq Research Fellowship Programme, 39–52.

an increase in gender-based violence (Amnesty International, 2009; Beghikani et al, 2010; Al-Ali & Pratt, 2011).

It is within this context that our team has been trying to study the specific problems and challenges facing female academics while also trying to build women and gender studies in Higher Education. Women make up a large percentage of both the student body and the teaching staff at universities; however, they are generally not involved in decision-making processes, nor in challenging discriminative practices and attitudes. Most academic women are too occupied with their professional and family responsibilities to try to change the existing system that reproduces social inequalities. Civil society organizations and individual activists advocating for women's rights tend to operate in isolation from academic institutions and vice versa, although some individual academics are also active in civil society (Al-Ali & Pratt, 2009).

Our research project uses gender as an analytical category describing the historically specific and contested social and cultural construction of what it means to be a man and woman. Gender in our research on female academics intersects with other social categories, such as class and generation to create, reproduce and challenge prevailing power relations. Across Iraqi society, there are wide ranging misconceptions and myths about the concept gender. The majority of Iraqis do not know the term. Those who have come across it, especially policy makers, religious authorities, civil society activists and even academics tend to associate gender with women only. This is the more harmless scenario, which is of course also common in other parts of the world, including western contexts. However, far more dangerous and damaging is the widespread association of gender with sexuality (gender is commonly translated as 'jins' which means sex), more particularly illicit sexual relations pertaining to homosexuality and extra-marital sex.

At the same time as our particular research topic and analytical framework is prone to misinterpretation and misunderstanding, we have been challenging and are challenged by our use of qualitative research methods. The long and deep-seated history of bias towards quantitative research is not unique to Iraq but common to many academic contexts in the Middle East. However, the specific history of isolation in Iraq due to dictatorship, wars, sanctions, and occupation, has not allowed for a close engagement with qualitative methods. It is not only logistic problems and the difficulty of establishing the kind of relationships of trust necessary for in depth qualitative research that has been a barrier. Most Iraqi social scientists continue to equate scientific research with value-free objective quantifiable data. By using women's narratives, their experiences and also our own perceptions of their and our lives within academia, we have been working against the foundations of what academia is supposed to be about.

All of us – Irada, Huda, Inass and Nadje – have written individual sections focusing on our personal experiences with the research project and the wider programme. We have jointly authored the introduction, which aimed to contextualize our personal reflections as well as our experiences as a team, which we will share in our conclusions.

NARRATING WOMEN'S LIVES

Irada Al-Jeboury

I was not blessed with the stories of my grandmothers. I only knew my grandmother on my father's side and I lost her when I was 7 years old. I don't retain much of her except those few hours when we used to visit her on special occasions and holidays to eat her delicious food. My grandfather enjoyed his life lying down, listening to songs on the radio, and getting my grandmother to do his bidding. I remember that she used to spend all her time in an effort to please him and avoid his anger. As for my grandmother on my mother's side, I have never even seen a picture of her. She died when she became sick after giving birth to her second child. My mother was only 2 years old and remembers nothing of her mother or of her brother who died only a few months later. All that my mother remembers of her mother are the stories told by the family. What stuck with me was my grandmother's desire to see a train. As she never had a chance to see one during her lifetime, she imagined it as she was lying on her sick bed.

I knew nothing about the world of stories and tales. I wrote my first words in anger when I was seven years old after my mother punished me unjustly. This was my first scream of protest against the authority of the family and the last time I didn't hide what I had written.

Since then, I have not stopped writing. When I was 17, I bid farewell to my words and my hidden notebooks after I lost my father in 1983 in the senseless war with Iran. The war ended after eight years, but my personal wars inside and outside the house went on. Journalism, which I took up in 1988, was a battleground of competition, my protest against the kind of literature and news that were published in a loud patriarchal voice. I did not want to lose the picture of my grandmother who was groping for peace by delaying her fights with my grandfather and died without gaining that peace, just as my grandmother on my mother's side died before she knew what a train looked like.

Women were present and active in the heart of the texts that I wrote, which were about the effects of wars on the structure of social relations. After 2003, escape from death was only by emigration (and this is another kind of death). Staying meant death was almost inevitable. Suspended between staying and leaving, I created a space in which I could stay and live by writing the stories of people I used to meet in the street or in the communal taxis: women on their way to the main morgue to look for their children, to the mass graves, or to the prisons. I began to write their stories so we would not lose the real voices of the country.

Through my communications with the Iraqi film director Maysoon Pachachi, I was introduced to Nadje Al-Ali who contacted me and invited me to be involved in this project. I got excited about it for a couple of reasons – the first was getting to know Nadje, since I had followed her work which seemed to be close to my own interests.

The idea of interviewing female academics of different generations and disciplines interested me. At first the work flowed, but as the days passed things became more and more difficult, for reasons of logistics: difficulties of moving around, the sudden closure of roads, the exposure to dangers of an unexpected kind. Before starting any interview I had to describe the research project in detail, the kinds of questions and why they were being asked, and I had to tell my interviewees about CARA, about Nadje Al-Ali, her books and her position towards the things that were happening in Iraq. Sometimes I used to spend an hour going through all this, and sometimes I used to find myself talking about my life more than the women I was interviewing were talking about theirs. Some interviews took more than a day, some a whole day, some half a day, and some had to be put together from separate interviews over a period of time. I completed some of my interviews over the Internet or on messenger, because I realized I was not going to be able to complete two of the interviews in the usual way for reasons to do with the interviewees' personal situations. On one occasion, I waited for one of the women for a whole day in my office, but she did not come and did not answer my phone calls. I remember the state of anxiety and fear I was in as I waited for her. The day of that interview was a difficult one, there were several explosions in different parts of Baghdad and I wondered if my interviewee had been wounded in one of these. It was difficult to complete this interview with this young academic. Two days later I found out through the colleague who had introduced me to her that she and her husband had had a disagreement and he had forbidden her to go to work for a few days.

Some of the women's lives lay like an open book in front of me and I used to read the lines, sometimes in grief and sometimes in joy. It happened that sometimes they saw me wiping away tears as I listened to the stories of what they had been through. I practiced trying to have the conversations without doing anything that would disturb or frighten them. I tried to listen without judging or blaming. I practiced the art of listening, which is very far away from our culture, as is this kind of research, which is new and strange and might make some people suspicious. Sometimes the women would answer readily and feel a sense of relief, but other times they were less willing and didn't want to dwell on what was painful. I learned to let things go, but sometimes without thinking I would find myself using my journalistic skills to come back to a point without it being hurtful.

The importance of listening and understanding is the most significant aspect these interviews taught me. They showed me a woman of my mother's age discovering for the first time in her life what was in her own soul without any pressure and from her own true desire. She thanked me as I was leaving that day, saying: 'Your questions to me have allowed a calm to return to my soul.'

I thought about my grandmother that day who perhaps was yearning for someone to listen to her story as were those women who I met by chance on the streets and in the communal taxis who appeared before me as I listened to the female academics of different ages, talking about their lives and their families and what they had lost and what they had given in order to be able to live their lives with dignity.

I had to find a way of doing the interviews without it affecting my own work at the university or my role as the mother of a 10-year old daughter who I was always anxious about. It was not easy to come to the workshops in Amman secretly with a child in tow, and without notifying the institution where I work in order not to provoke resentment from colleagues who envy anyone to go abroad for a conference even if it is not related to their field.

The picture of my grandmother that I remember, and that of my other grandmother who dreamt of seeing the train, and my daughter's questions about why I am taking part in such work, and the women whose stories have been made to disappear by the wars and the embargos of all sorts, prevent me from losing hope.

The challenge of losing hope has motivated me share my ideas with my classes, which contain young male and female students who largely did not experience but voices of aircrafts, bombings, car explosions, and sanctions. I started bringing media texts to my students and address questions that are considered 'shocking' according to current social norms and the general cultural context: questions about self-images, the image and representation of others, stereotypes, the structure of patriarchal society, social roles of gender and their relationship to laws and authority. I have been examining these questions by first looking at media sources, and then deconstructing them.

With the end of each academic year, I realize that the tunnel is still long, but the hope on some of the students' faces as they proceed to complete their degrees or apply for certain professions in the media institutions assures me that there is a light at the end that will illuminate the path of Iraq towards peace and justice.

A POLITICAL SCIENTIST'S JOURNEY

Inass Al-Enezy

I had no interest in women's issues or gender studies before starting this project. I attribute that to several reasons: first, I was born into and grew up in a family, which did not discriminate between children based on their gender. Secondly, I am not a very sociable person and tend to isolate myself. This has limited my interactions with others and did not enable me to grasp their suffering and problems. Thirdly, in terms of my religious beliefs, I always thought that God created people equally, endowed them their rights, and guided them in terms of their duties and responsibilities within their respective communities.

After having engaged with the project about the specific problems and challenges facing Iraqi female academics and the opportunity it gave me to meet and talk with women, I was really shocked by what the women told me, which opened my eyes to the magnitude of the tragedy women have been facing. Iraqi society witnessed many wars, during which women experienced an extraordinary and unique situation: they had a leading role in society in all aspects of life while many men were absent fighting the various wars. I assumed this situation allowed women to recognize their own abilities and would allow them to say: 'We are here!' But what happened was the opposite, even after the change of the political regime. Despite the fact that Iraqi people have been discontent with all political parties and politicians, they have preferred to elect men instead of women. The only thing that helped women was the 'quota' system that stipulates 25% representation for women in all political bodies.

When I spoke with female academics about the political situation, specifically the elections, I could sense that many women lack political independence. I had seen this before: when I was a manager of an election centre in Baghdad, I noticed that most women came to the election Centre with a man from the family, and he appeared to have influence over her political choices.

Based on these experiences and the contents of my interviews with female academics, I realize now what I omitted before, namely that men and women experience things, particularly with respect to wars and its aftermaths, differently. During war times, man strives just for survival, especially when he knows that these wars are in vain. Meanwhile, woman strives for others, the family and society more widely. In this context, Iraqi female academics gained a unique position. Over a long time they worked hard and kept academia going, secured their families and provided them with a decent life. They have fought on many fronts.

But in the aftermaths of wars, I have discovered that there is a complex and troublesome situation female academics face. Men want to restore their positions as master in the house and as the boss at work. They are busy trying to regain what they consider to be their natural rights. Meanwhile, female academics experience paradoxical feelings and situations. On the one hand, they may be feeling tired, exhausted and in need of some rest, because even the warrior sometimes needs to leave the battlefield, lie in the shade of a verdant tree and enjoy peace for a while. But, on the other hand, they also feel compelled to fight to keep what they have gained over a period of time.

In light of what I have learned and concluded from my in depth reading of the interviews with female academics, I can say that the project has given me the opportunity to understand what gender means and to what extent I had an incomplete understanding and imagination about this topic. I had always conceived of gender in term of duties, responsibilities and rights, but what about feelings, dreams, and desires? Perhaps someone will say that feelings, dreams, and desires are all contained within rights, but what I mean here and search for is slightly different: to take the responsibilities seriously, to do the duties keenly, to express the rights correctly and defend them strongly. This is what gender means, the law of rights and the soul of humanity.

When I got involved with the IRFP project, I did not expect that it would change me to the extent it did. Travelling and communicating with people from around the world and being introduced to other cultures, to develop experiences, all this has a brilliant impact on the psychology of human beings. I felt personally that it made me interact with my environment more positively, which ultimately will allow me to give more back to my society. My hope is that the project will expand and continue to open doors for new generation of outstanding academics, so that they will be able to experience what I benefited from.

More recently, CARA and Nadje have given me the opportunity to attend two courses in the UK, one at the SOAS Centre for Gender Studies, and the other one at Nottingham University about international human rights law. These two courses very much depended on applied and qualitative research including the analysis of case studies and documents. Previously I had always focused on theoretical literature and research, so this opened up new fields and possibilities for me. However, I should stress that it is not easy to carry out empirical research in an unsafe, insecure, and non-trusting environment, where people might refuse to talk to strangers, and perhaps do not always provide the correct information. Gaining the confidence of my respondents was a big challenge to me during the interviewing process.

Despite this fact, I intend to go ahead and pursue these new qualitative methods and ideas. When I was lecturing at my college in Baghdad, I did not like the traditional way of imparting knowledge to students. However, there were many obstacles in my way when I tried to make some changes in my teaching style. I wanted to give students cutting-edge materials and urge them to discuss them in class. I also encouraged them to find meanings of political idioms in English as I felt that these would help them in their future careers. But the bureaucratic control within universities is reluctant to accept any changes that might require internal reform. Many students refuse it on their part because traditional methods of teaching provide ready recipes to them to pass and graduate without significant effort. After I attended seminars in the UK and saw the additional events that students participate in, like films, presentations, discussions and conferences. I became more determined to achieve the change, which I aspire to. Even though I know that change will not be easy to achieve in Iraqi universities. Yet I believe that I am now a different person, armed with knowledge to be strong enough to face any problem. I have always believed in change, now this belief has grown. I think the friction with different people and the opportunity to learn about the experiences of others gives any one of us the chance to change toward the better. This is what IRFP has given to me.

Last but not least, I have to return to the personal matter that I mentioned above, which is that I have always been prone to isolate myself. These days I have come to realize that even if isolation was a personal choice, it cannot be the only and best choice, especially if I want to move forward and utilize the lessons and experiences of life. Language is the tool of contact between human beings. During these past months, I often wished that my English was better in order to make more positive contact with different professors and students, and learn from their lessons and experiences.

Ironically, in spite of my tendency to seek isolation and feel homesick whenever I travelled, I always hated borders between countries because they limit people and divide them. Today I believe that borders do not prevent positive interaction between peoples as long as they relate to each other and support each other. This is what real freedom means. The range of diversity in students' nationalities at British universities has surprised me. This confirms that academia unites people under one roof and gives them the opportunity to communicate and interact.

I would like to take this opportunity to express my thanks and gratitude to all who gave me this chance to get out from limited to unlimited scopes, from physical limits to the space of humanity. As my experience with IRFP benefited me greatly on a personal level, I can imagine the extent to which the project as whole may refresh Iraqi academia if many of the new generation of academics will have similar opportunities. We need to identify and support our outstanding students to create an open-minded generation that has interaction with the outside world and takes responsibility to revive Higher Education in Iraq.

RESEARCHING GENDER AMONGST REFUGEE ACADEMICS

Huda Al-Dujaili

In 2006, when the sectarian violence was at its peak, and violence against women increased, especially in terms of kidnapping, I found it difficult as a single woman to keep my 19 years old daughter safe. I decided to leave Baghdad and take my daughter to Amman. There I had many Iraqi friends, who, I was hoping, could be helpful in need. Up to now, the situation has not changed sufficiently to encourage me to return to Iraq.

Living in Amman meant living in peace for my daughter and me. We socialized with many Iraqi friends, which made our life easier. But at the same time I had, all of a sudden, been pulled away from my career as a university lecturer and scholar. This was very painful and stressful for me.

Working with CARA was my golden opportunity since it enabled me to mingle with people who shared my professional background and interests. This experience was useful for me on many levels: it helped me to return to my career and to engage with Iraqi academics, international scholars and intellectuals. But it also helped me to regain my self-confidence, and the feeling that I could still work for my country even if I was based outside Iraq.

The research project about Iraqi female academics enhanced my existing research skills and introduced me to a new subject area. In the Iraqi context, the field of economic development has not been linked to gender studies at all. However, my previous experience as a civil society activist, promoting human rights and women's empowerment, led me to realize that Iraqi society was not practicing human rights in everyday life, and particularly when it comes to women's rights. This recognition had pushed me to work as a trainer in human rights with a special emphasis on women's rights.

In addition to learning more about gender as an analytical category for research, the CARA-funded project also introduced me to qualitative research methods. This was a totally new technique for me, since I had only used quantitative method in my previous research. Generally speaking, qualitative methods are not commonly used in the social sciences in Iraq. When Nadje introduced us to qualitative methods, like informal in- depth interviews or participant observation, for example, I was sceptical at first but then realized that these methods can help us identify complex factors such as social norms, socio-economic status, ascribed social roles and attitudes.

Participating in a team was a very useful experience that was also new for me in the context of academia. We have been exchanging the work done by each of us, and, with the help of each other's comments, have been able to learn from each other's strengths and weaknesses. This participatory process of learning has benefitted all of us. I also felt that we benefited from Nadje's research expertise in relation to Iraqi women as well as her personal experiences as someone with Iraqi connections herself. I feel that the continuous discussion and the increased awareness of our research methods and content facilitated my work and helped to push me forward not only with respect to this project, but also on a more general level.

Another extremely useful dimension of the CARA Iraq fellowship were the workshops with other research teams. These workshops enabled contact with other researchers across a range of different disciplines. We discussed issues in subject areas very far from my own sphere of expertise and experience, which enlarged my vision and scope of thinking. At the same time, our team managed to get the views of other workshop participants on our research and gender issues more widely in Iraq. This helped our team as we were forced to consider other peoples' views and perceptions. At the same time, I also think that our team managed to challenge some of the preconceptions and stereotypes about women and gender prevalent amongst our colleagues.

My specific challenge as a team member based in Amman was to find Iraqi female academics, who had left the country for one reason or another, and were now living in Jordan. Yet finding them was not the most difficult challenge, as I sometimes found it hard to persuade them to be part of my research sample. Why was that so? Iraqi refugees tend to avoid Iraqis they do not know well when it comes to discussing certain issues, especially those touching on politics, ethnicity, religion and social class background. I think we Iraqis still suffer from the same fears that were instilled in us before 2003. Also after 2003, our priority has been to stay safe, whether we were inside Iraq or outside, always fearing that criticizing the system may cause problems to us. My understanding of this situation helped me gain the trust and acceptance of most of my interviewees, while in some cases I was refused.

Another aspect that proved to be challenging for me was the time commitment. I did not expect that conducting interviews would be so time consuming. I had to be flexible according to the time of my interviewees. Many of them were working, so I had to arrange my time according to their free time. On several occasions I received last minute phone calls asking me to postpone the meeting. It also became clear in the early phase of my research that one meeting would not be sufficient. I first had to establish a relationship and trust before I could actually start asking questions. And while my first set of interviews were rather short and not much in depth, I learned from Nadje and the other team members how to conduct more in depth interviews. These elicit more interesting information but certainly take much more time than just going through a list of questions.

Introducing myself as an Iraqi female researcher working on gender issues was very significant to my interviewees and to myself. From my point of view I started to enjoy getting more insights into gender-focused research as it started to help me understand some of the social problems that my country suffers from. For example, I became more aware about the relationships between women and men, and the changing relationship of the state to gender relations. I also realized that gender is an entry point into many broader issues related to politics, society, history, and culture.

As for the female academics I was talking to, once convinced to talk to me, they all welcomed the subject and ended up being happy in participating. As a result of these contacts, I not only learned a lot about the situation of my colleagues in Amman and their lives previously in Iraq, but I also managed to enlarge my circle of friends. I started to understand the situation of the Iraqi female academics from different angles, such as the significance of the family in terms of their personalities, especially the role of fathers who often have a profound impact on their daughters, but I also realized how flexible and adaptable many of the women I had spoken to were in relation to rapidly changing outside conditions, like war and sanctions. Looking again at the interviews of women of different generations, what I see clearly in front of me is the important role female academics have played over time and across different generations and backgrounds.

Finally, I continue to benefit greatly from the encounter with regional scholars who are part of a growing network of women and gender studies academics, as well as women's rights activists. Now that I met women who have many years of experience working in the field, I feel inspired to help facilitate it in my country as well. For myself, I have regained my passion for research and have been introduced to a new discipline that I would like to explore further and contribute to with my own research.

In my view, IRFP has already started in preparing the foundations for capacity and the infrastructure for research amongst Iraqi academics. It has helped to both broaden and deepen current research capacity and agendas. In terms of women and gender studies, the project has introduced a discipline and concepts that were largely absent from Iraqi academia. I hope we will be able to pursue this to deepen our understanding and research potential. Other colleagues have managed to gain new insights and tools for research to already existing disciplines and subjects.

ENGENDERING KNOWLEDGE

Nadje Al-Ali

Before getting involved in the CARA IRFP, I had been researching and publishing on women and gender issues in relation to Iraq. Having studied the modern history of Iraqi women as well as the impact of the invasion in 2003 and the Occupation (Al-Ali, 2005, 2007, 2009), I was aware of the difficult living conditions for Iraqi women. At the same time, my encounters with Iraqi academics, who had to flee Iraq post-2003, made me aware of the crisis of Higher Education and the many challenges Iraqi academics were facing. In 2008, I started a fellowship and mentoring programme for female academic refugees at SOAS that brought me into regular contact with my colleagues from Iraq. Although it was open to refugee academics of all national backgrounds, the majority of women we have been hosting so far have been from Iraq due to the scale of the violence and crisis not only facing Higher Education but society more generally.

One of the Iraqi fellows, Dr Sawsan al-Assaf, had been particularly active in trying to raise awareness about the problems and risks for Iraqi academics. The two of us decided to apply to the first round of CARA's IRFP with a project that was dear to both of our hearts. Unfortunately Sawsan was prevented from participating in the project due to immigration issues, which took a couple of years to sort out. Both of us felt incredibly frustrated and upset at the time but we also knew that we were tied by legal restrictions. With the help of friends and CARA's contacts, we were able to create our current team that has been working together since December 2009.

Throughout the project there have been tensions for me in terms of my roles as Principal Investigator with research and writing experience and a very busy schedule, feeling compelled to move the project in the most efficient and quick way, and my role as capacity-builder, wanting to share my skills and experiences and hoping for the team members to take charge and control of specific aspects of the project. It took a couple of workshops in Amman before all team members started to take ownership of the project and were able to speak about and for it with greater confidence. Over the past months, I have sensed that with every task completed, with every workshop attended, each team member has become more involved, more confident and also competent in terms of the task at hand.

Language and gender issues have been coming into play as some of the discussions with the larger group were dominated by the international principal investigators and Iraqi male participants. As a feminist scholar specialized in women and gender issues in the Middle East and as a women's rights activist, I am sensitive to some of the apparent power dynamics emanating from gender and generation, but also Iraqi versus 'western' scholars. Gendered dynamics emerged not only in terms of who was speaking and who was representing whom but also in terms of the appropriation of space and constructions of hierarchies of knowledge production. These are not unique features to Iraqi or Middle Eastern cultures as I have also experienced very similar patterns in British Higher Education where women have remained marginal to managerial and decision-making posts. Given these dynamics I also felt a tension in terms of my own positionality as a female academic, wanting to speak out and disrupt male prevalence, and as an academic based in a privileged western institution, in a country that has been involved in the Occupation of Iraq. Not wanting to reproduce relationships imbued with colonial undertones, I found this tension occasionally difficult and painful.

One very concrete skill I have been trying to pass on and develop amongst the team members is that of informal in-depth interviews as one specific research method of wider qualitative research. Irada, Huda and Inass did not need to be convinced that studying the specific problems and challenges of their colleagues in Iraq and Jordan would not generate statistics as much as qualitative data. Or to put it differently, trying to quantify the problems and challenges that female academics are facing within Higher Education in Iraq might be a starting point for a large scale survey. Yet, given the scope of our small research team we would not have been able to generate a large enough sample to make quantitative research meaningful. More importantly, however, we wanted to find out about women's experiences, attitudes and feelings as much as the objective conditions they are facing within Iraqi universities.

Not surprisingly, our team was confronted with reactions along a continuum of bemusement and admonishment and an underlying perception that we were engaged in 'unscientific' work. I was not new to the perception common amongst many of my research students from the Middle East that credible research needs to be quantifiable into numbers and statistics. Here, I do not want to belabour the debates around quantitative versus qualitative methods, which have a long history within the social sciences and have been widely written about. But I would like to suggest that in the Iraqi context 'truth' and 'objectivity' are far more than epistemological debates about knowledge production within academia.

Contestations about Iraq's past, questions about the nature of the Iraqi state in the making, citizenship and belonging as well as the kind of society Iraqis want to strive for are frequently fought and argued over with the objectivity card, not acknowledging the fact that different Iraqis might have experienced the past and the present differently and might have varying visions for its future. Ethnicity and religion are only aspects of the huge variety and range of Iraqi experiences and attitudes. As I have argued elsewhere (2007), class, gender, place of residence, profession and generation used to be far more significant markers of difference until quite recently. At the same time, I have also been acutely aware that postmodern relativism taken to the extreme to an 'anything goes' is not good enough in a context where many people have lost their lives through dictatorship, sanctions, wars and invasion. It has been challenging in my own work and in working with the team to straddle the balance between recognizing the significance of people's positionalities in constructing memories, experiences and knowledge while also striving to obtain information about 'what really happened and is happening'.

I see my own aspirations and potential contribution to help rebuilding Higher Education in Iraq as effectively channelled through the IRFP model. It has enabled me to support female and male academics in Iraq who are interested in introducing women or gender studies into the curriculum and teaching agendas as well as sensitize academics in other disciplines to gender issues. On a larger scale, I am hoping that my work with the IRFP will help to strengthen the social sciences by building research capacities, introducing innovative teaching and research methods, and facilitating networks of Iraqi, regional and international academics.

CONCLUSION

Working as a team on the research project about Iraqi female academics and participating in the CARA IRFP and RRT workshops has clearly been transformative to all of us, both on personal but also collective levels. Writing this joint chapter, we realized how much we have developed as a team but also how much the team has moved us individually and our thinking forward. While the interactions amongst the four of us were generally tension-free and harmonious, even if sometimes challenging, the interactions with the larger group participating in IRFP workshops were often more difficult. We already mentioned some of the issues earlier, such as gender dynamics between male and female academics, especially amongst the Iraqi participants. It was clear from some of the comments and jokes that we as 'the gender team' were not always taken entirely serious by our colleagues. At the same time, we referred to prevailing attitudes towards the social sciences by our colleagues from the natural sciences, especially when it comes to qualitative research that is generally perceived to not fit the criteria of 'objective science'. Unwittingly, yet, not surprisingly, we occasionally found ourselves on the defensive during plenary discussions. As time moved on, and as we become more confident with our work, so our interactions with the wider group became more assertive and relaxed. And fortunately we all have a good sense of humour as well!

Another source of tension relates to the very topic we have been studying. While none of us would ever seriously claim academic insights into tuberculosis detection or the use of mobile devices for diabetic patients, all Iraqi project participants had preconceived ideas and strong views related to the situation of Iraqi women and gender relations more generally, and the situation and challenges facing female Iraqi academics more specifically. The discussions around our project occasionally became platforms for ideological and political positions and discussions. This situation was also apparent with our colleagues in other social science projects, particularly the project on the representation of national identity, religion and gender in primary school text books. Although these ideological positions were distracting from our concerns at times, we appreciated that the IRFP workshop provided a relatively safe space to discuss sensitive and taboo issues within Iraqi society.

Overall, our team enjoyed the contact with colleagues, both western and from Iraq, who work not only in different fields in the social sciences but also in the natural sciences. It is almost impossible in our regular academic lives to mingle with colleagues in the natural sciences. We all found these encounters and the discussions that emerged between us to be very interesting and thought provoking. The role of the Facilitators was crucial here as they played a positive role in enabling constructive discussions across participants speaking very different languages and pursuing radically different projects and methods.

More recently, we have also been involved in the establishment of a regional network of women and gender studies scholars and women's rights activists. CARA's Regional Round Table (RRT) model allowed us to meet with other colleagues from Iraq who share our interests and concerns and who, like us, would like to facilitate in creating capacity for research and teaching. Given the on-going security crisis and difficulty of getting around, it is not easy for scholars based at different universities in Iraq to meet with each other. In addition to making connections between academics inside Iraq, we enjoyed meeting our colleagues from Lebanon, Turkey, Palestine, Jordan and Egypt who have been involved over the past decade in setting up women and gender studies programmes and centres at various universities in the region. These regional exchanges, which have been taken place in Amman and Beirut, have also involved Iraqi and other regional women's rights activists. We realized that in Iraq, as elsewhere in the world, there is a strong synergy and connection between those struggling for greater gender equality and social justice and those working within academia on gender issues.

REFERENCES

Amnesty International (2008) *Trapped by Violence. Women in Iraq.* http://www.amnesty.org/en/library/asset/MDE14/005/2009/en/e6cda898-fa16-4944-af74-f3efc0cf6a4d/mde140052009en.pdf (accessed 15 September 2011).

Al-Ali, N., & Pratt, N. (2011) *Conspiracy of Near Silence: Violence against Iraqi Women. Middle East Report* (MERIP), *258*, pp. 34–37.

Al-Ali, N., & Pratt, N. (2009) *What kind of Liberation? Women and the Occupation of Iraq.* Berkeley: University of California Press.

Al-Ali, N. (2007) *Iraqi Women: Untold Stories from 1948 to the Present.* London & New York: Zed Books.

Al-Ali, N. (2005) Gendering Reconstruction: Iraqi Women between Dictatorship, Wars, Sanctions and Occupation. *Third World Quarterly, 26*(4–5), 739–758.

Beghikani, N., Gill, A., Hague, G., &Ibraheem, K. (2010) *Honor-Based Violence and Honor Killings in Iraqi Kurdistan and in the Kurdish Diaspora in the United Kingdom* (Bristol, November 2010).

4. A JOURNEY OF LEARNING:THE CURRICULUM IN IRAQI SCHOOLS AND HIGHER EDUCATION

INTRODUCTION

The aim of this project is to analyze the school curriculum of post-invasion Iraq, and to examine whether it satisfies the aims of advocates for educational change, namely that the school curriculum becomes non-ideological and objective. However in the process of carrying out this research I have also reflected on the Social Science curriculum of Higher Education and the status of the research it produces. The main focus of this chapter is twofold: the first is an exploration of the social, political and epistemological difficulties of carrying out social science research which takes the school education system as its object; the second is my difficulties in explaining the politics of research in Iraq to a CARA audience.

Since the founding of the modern Iraqi state in 1921, education has been based on the central idea that it can be a major factor in unifying Iraqi culture. In building the nation state in Iraq the strategy of King Faisal I (1921–1933) was based on two pillars: education and military service. He wrote in his memoir that he wanted to create a 'people that we refine, train and teach'. Because of the nature of the emerging state with regard to the political affiliations of the elites and the ideological orientations of those in charge of education strategies, a single interpretation was imposed with respect to the most sensitive issues, namely the religious and historical education curricula.

The curriculum was built on the base of the identity of the Sunni State, with an attempt to overcome differences of an ethnic and sectarian nature. But this attempt did not succeed, and the history of modern education has witnessed a lot of conflict because of this. Despite the declared aims of education policies, the curriculum strengthened divisions, and instilled a sense of marginalization and confrontation with state/power ideology for some groups. The Iraqi memory is still not able to produce a common history: it is fragmented between many corpuses belonging to four centuries of official history and the parallel experience which reacts against it. There is little attempt to re-think this history and to surpass the mythology that has produced it. I argue that this history should not be viewed as a text that describes a reality, but as speech which must be conceptualized as a political, social and cultural product.

In 2003 UNESCO described the status of education in Iraq as having reached the level of a farce, and that it could not provide the solutions to political and social issues. At that moment the Occupation represented the hope in many quarters for a

H. Brunskell-Evans & M. Moore (Eds.), Reimagining Research for Reclaiming the Academy in Iraq: Identities and Participation in Post-Conflict Enquiry: The Iraq Research Fellowship Programme, 53–63.

dramatic transformation in the education system. The question which has not subsequently been asked however, but one which I ask, is whether there has been a real epistemological shift from the traditional curriculum seen as ideological, normative and expressing 'one voice'. Are we in fact maintaining the same traditional paradigm, one dependent on a specific balance of forces, especially the Islamic parties' dominance on the political scene, and their insistence on holding the portfolio of the Ministry of Education?

FINDING A TEAM

The main problem I faced in developing this research was how to find a team of social scientists for this task which would be conversant with CARA's requirements and conditions. Higher Education in Iraq has suffered, in the last twenty years, from a significant reduction of investment in the Social Sciences with regard to both scientific endeavour and human potential.

As far as I was concerned I could form a team consisting of four persons: Irada Al-Joboury, Jawad Al-Tamimy, Juma'a Abdalla and myself. We had all worked together in different previous projects, and there was a possibility to ask other academics to join the main team to do the interviews about school curricula with teachers in four different Iraqi governorates. In the end the project and the composition of this team was accepted by the IRFP with the addition of Professor Roger Slee from the Institute of Education, The University of London, UK as the principal investigator.

Unfortunately Kate Robertson, the Executive Director of the IRFP, was obliged to inform me later that I should replace my colleague Irada Al-Joboury because she was to become involved with another team within the IRFP concerned with the status of female Iraqi academics in Higher Education. I was obliged to look for another person to complete the team but this was not an easy task, because Irada was supposed to cover the subject of the image of women in Iraqi school curricula. I felt that I had lost my 'winning card': Irada is one of the best scholars who dealt with this subject in Iraq; in addition we had previously worked well together as a 'team' rather than as individual researchers. Looking for a team member who is an academic, a researcher, and a specialist free from any prejudice is like looking for a needle in the straw. These characteristics are very rare and are seldom found in Iraqi universities nowadays.

SOCIAL SCIENCE RESEARCH METHODOLOGY

One of the difficulties of finding social science researchers is the absence of training in Social Science research methodologies in Iraqi universities. The building blocks of Iraq's universities date back to the 1908 when the first academic institutions – a teacher's training institute and a law school – were established to supply a fledgling Iraqi state with administrators and jurists. The first purpose for the Higher Education system in Iraq was to produce 'governmental employees' rather than a knowledge community. This philosophy is still dominant today where the university teacher's main task is teaching not research. There are about 32,214 academics in the academic year 2010\2011, but very few of them could be described as researchers.

The lack of the subject 'social science research methodology' is one of the most prominent weaknesses that have governed the social sciences in the Iraqi universities. Through our extrapolation of the rules of curriculum in social science departments, we found there is no course named 'methodology'. There is, however, one required course that devotes one aspect to the methodology of scientific research, or research methods, usually taking up to two hours of one week. This situation includes all Iraqi universities, because curriculum items are centrally planned from Iraqi Ministry of Higher Education. Indeed, in some colleges and departments such as law schools or colleges of Management and Economy there is not a single course in methodology either for undergraduates or for postgraduate students. There is a unique exception at the University of Baghdad with regard to statistics where there is a course called 'Designing Surveys – Survey Design', and a Section of Industrial Management at the Faculty of Management and Economics, where we find 'The Assets of Scientific Research' for one term when it is very necessary for the student to carry out research in order to graduate.

The near total absence of Research Methodology in Iraqi universities can be explained, in part, by the philosophy of Higher Education that graduates don't need research skills because Iraq at this stage needs staff not researchers contributing elements in a knowledge society. The courses studied by both undergraduates and postgraduates where we can find the term Methodology included in the curriculum of the Social Sciences generally aim to teach technical tools, such as how to select a subject, building the literature search, how to refer to the sources, and so on. This produces students who do not differentiate between terms such as: 'introduction' and 'conclusion', 'induction' and 'deduction', 'description' and 'interpretation', and the difference between 'quantitative' and 'quantitative methods'.The social science faculties at Iraqi universities are still dealing with the issue of method as an instrument, and not a specialized scientific field, so it is taught in the first or second year as part of the necessary introductive tools for the student.

CARA FIRST MEETING: A LOT OF RESENTMENT

The first meeting of the IRFP assembled four successful teams who had been awarded CARA grants, as well as Principal Investigators and the Facilitators. This was a valuable opportunity to get acquainted and to exchange ideas on the four projects. Our project, which is an analysis of education curricula in Iraq, seemed to interest all the participants. It was received by many as 'a political issue', but it was not the proposal of the project which created this impression, but because of the nature of the discourse used by the team members when they tried to define the project and the ideas beyond it. In particular we emphasized how the problem of education in Iraq has been part of Iraqi society's problems since the foundation of modern Iraq in 1921. Thus the participants were prompted to engage with ideas about historical backgrounds and to think about the relationship to the existing political conflict in Iraq today, with all the impacts on the education curriculum, and the relationship between curriculum and state-building that this entails.

Some of the participants were suspicious that there was an underlying previous attitude of the researchers involved in the project which is not consistent with the standards of scientific research. This prompted the Principal Investigator, to say: 'if we want to make research and not a political manifesto, we must return to the research norms'. Another query was raised about the schedule of the project and whether it would extend beyond the designated time-scale and thus beyond the budget as well. As for the proposal of the project, it also encountered some criticism, and perhaps most important of all was the comment by one of the Facilitators who said that if he had been responsible for assessing projects submitted to CARA he wouldn't have given our project the grant. He argued that the project 'deals with important questions, but the draft was not written correctly'. Of course, not without some attempt to show 'sympathy' with us as the 'trapped' residents of Iraq he emphasized the different perspectives of the researchers within the team even though we had agreement about the topic of research, and he pointed to his concerns that we were raising personal biases.

The meeting also included a lot of debates about the status of education curricula in areas of conflict, and about the major powers in those conflicts who could determine the nature of curriculum within a divided community, and of course the issue of the impact on the population of integrating a curriculum in certain ways. The meeting also discussed how, as researchers, we formulated questions on our proposed questionnaires to teachers, given the potential conflicts of carrying out research in such a situation. The most important conclusion we took away with us from these explicit and direct confrontations is that we Iraqi academics were in need to open up our discourse to international, Western academics. Because our Principal Investigator was strict regarding the requirements of the research, we sent him a revised version of our research proposal, when he insisted that his comments were not a strictness belonging to him, but a result of his adherence to strict criteria: 'Methodology and methods are key areas in a proposal in our academic culture' he said.

My own way of understanding this is that there was an underlying mistrust of our team's capacity for carrying out valid research within Western criteria. I suggest this view has a history and emerges from imperialism. Lord Cromer (1841–1917), the Victorian-Edwardian imperialist who was a British Consul-General of Egypt where he served the interests of Britain particularly well, wrote that he had been particularly influenced by what Sir Alfred Lyall (1835–1911), a British civil servant in India, and a literary historian and poet had once told him. Cromer (1908) informs us Lyall had advised 'Accuracy is abhorrent to the oriental mind'.

THE SPECTRA OF ANTONIO GRAMSCI, PIERRE BOURDIEU AND EDWARD SAID

Having described above some of the criticisms made of our research project it is important to stress that our Principal Investigator, when we met for the first time, was keen to be an interlocutor rather than a supervisor of research. We talked at length about the situation in Iraq and the Occupation. We also discussed the possible contribution of Edward Said's (1996) Representations of the Intellectual and Pierre Bourdieu's (Bourdieu and Passeron 1990) thesis about education, and our Principal Investigator was keen to support our wish that these texts become some of the theoretical and intellectual resources for analyzing our research data. He talked without any arrogance or attempt to exercise the role of the teacher, although he continued to be doubtful, as others in fact, of our hypothesis that the changing curriculum is ideological. He insisted we must 'look at education policy, not politics in education'. We are not sure whether the long dialogues with him eventually dispelled some of his uncertainty but nevertheless we continued to follow the maxim of Thomas Mann (1875–1955) the German novelist, short story writer, social critic, philanthropist, and essayist who allegedly insisted 'Everything is Politics'.

Antonio Gramsci (1975: 265) argues 'science' itself is 'political activity and political thought, as long as it changes people, makes them different than they were before'. It is not necessary to distinguish between 'policy in the sense of philosophy on the one hand, and politics as the politics in the narrow sense of the other'. This artificial distinction is important to recognize especially if we deal with an important topic in Iraq such as education. Gramsci's definition of the state is 'the compound of practical activities and the theory which justifies control and maintains it, and even enables the ruling class to gain satisfaction from their control'(1975:261). It is natural that education should be an integral part of political science as at the same it means in the end, 'the science of the state '. In fact Gramsci emphasizes what he calls 'educational or formative' role of the state and said that we must indeed look to the State as 'educator'. As the educator it works to unite all individuals/citizens in a kind of 'human collective'. The educative pressure works on each individual separately, to help him/ her to gain satisfaction and to co-operate, 'thus transforming the political to the cultural, and the relationship of hegemony to rational and non- coercive consent' (1975:265). Thus even though the state takes responsibility for the infrastructure to education, this 'does not mean leaving factors to develop arbitrarily'... The state is a tool for 'rationalization' (1975: 267).

In the context of distinguishing between the political community and civil society, Gramsci speaks about the stage when a religious authority moves from the subsidiary level of civil society to the primary level of government , that is, when this religious authority itself becomes part of the state, setting up conflict between the secular civil society , and the state/religious authority. This religious authority becomes part of the political community, and is monopolized by a distinctive group which controls the religious authority to maintain power for themselves (1975: 265).

The injunction not to get involved in politics, and the assumption that knowledge can be pure, not political, are ideals. Edward Said (1979:4) says 'The researcher is not necessarily separated from reality, and he is consciously or unconsciously involved in a set of beliefs, and into a social status (ref).He goes on to say 'there is not, after all, a non- political knowledge'. Policies for education where there is no differentiation between the state and the overwhelming presence of religious parties dominating the political scene means the existence of multiculturalism always comes to the surface as conflict rather than a mutual recognition.

Bourdieu (1990: 4) concurs with Said and insists that 'of all the oppositions that artificially divide social science, the most fundamental, and the most ruinous is the one that is set up between subjectivism and objectivism'. Although he uses the French education system as his example I argue his thesis applies to the cultural context of Iraq. He argues that the French educational system reproduces the cultural division of society, and that all pedagogic action is a kind of symbolic violence practiced by arbitrary power to impose a cultural identity. He insists 'every power which manages to impose meaning and to impose them as legitimate by concealing the power relations which are the basis of its force, adds its own specifically symbolic force to those power relations' (op cit.).

RESEARCHERS TALK FROM THE FIELD

Numerous other researchers became involved in the project to complement the initial team by going out into the field and collecting data from teachers working in four governorates of Iraq. They describe their experiences here:

Dr. Hamed Jasim: Karbala Governorate

The city of Karbala is the most important Shiite city in Iraq and in the world as well, although the city of Najaf is the seat of Shiite thought and historically a settler for Shiite Science as it is known. The city of Karbala began competing with Najaf in this standing after the U.S. Occupation. This led the clergy to seek to go to extremes in declaring the religious aspect of the city by spreading the religious culture, religious schools and mosques into the city, accompanied by an attempt to exclude everyone who disagreed with these procedures either directly or indirectly. We could add an important dimension in describing the cultural management of the province. There is collusion between the dominant political line and a particular religious line, which has turned into an alliance. This integration is portrayed as one unit: what is political is religious and what is religious is political. This threshold is built with sufficient solidity to change the views of all who live within that framework, tying the direction of this threshold. This correlation is reflected in all city life, and most clearly in the educational institutions. Thus, we found that the fear factor controls the majority of interviewees, despite my continuous confirmations that I will not mention the interviewee's name or place of business. This assurance was not enough to reduce this fear, because the teacher is aware that in the event of leakage of any information which may disagree with the general line this could lead to his dismissal.

Dr. Hazim al-Nuaimi: The Governorate of Baghdad/Karkh

The most difficult task to complete the interviews was to get approval from schools for the teachers to be interviewed. So, from the beginning, with the help of my acquaintances, I confined my interviewees to their relatives and neighbours: men, women and female students and students from area schools. I also looked for how to reach them outside school, because I decided from the beginning that I will not visit schools and meet with teachers there in order not to embarrass them and as a result they may refuse the interview. I also decided that I would complete the meeting in my house or their house or a mediator's house. This, I hoped, would guarantee that answers were more objective. In order that the interviewee could talk freely and give his or her opinion credibly and clearly without fear or hesitation, I was forced to reassure them at length, making clear the subject of research and explaining the larger aim or the project beyond the individual interview.

Some of those interviewed were hesitant and doubtful, and haunted by the anxiety of saying their opinions for fear of being accused of sectarianism, or subjected to sanctions or anger from the administration of the school or the Ministry of Education. In particular they didn't know me personally, so I had had to reassure them in various styles and talk about the general situation. Others were brave or excited against the changes and were not interested in what might happen after expressing their opinions. Interestingly the unwary were Shiites, not Sunnis. I had noticed also that female teachers were more audacious than male teachers.

I had noticed fear among respondents at the beginning of the meeting, so I had asked each of them if they were afraid to make the interview. Some of them clearly believed that fear pervades in all aspects of our lives and not just fear from administrative sanctions. It was clear that the fear here was of sectarian issues, so some tried to be very neutral when justifying their answers. The main concern of most of the interviewed was not to create clashes and conflicts within the school or with the departments. They sought to alleviate the problems to religious changes in the curriculum only within narrow limits avoiding impact on the other affiliations. It is natural that such a position to keep things pending and unresolved will generate many problems with educational work, especially since many of the respondents stated that they do not teach or focus on topics that collide with the students' perceptions or affiliations.

Dr. AbdAlwahed Meshal: Anbar Governorate

Teachers are acting their roles, through a real confrontation with the religious authorities who have now become the real actor in changing the terms of the curriculum. Some teachers believe that this intervention in the development of curricula is unacceptable, especially since the imposed changes are obligatory. There is a difference in the nature of reactions however: we have found that those who hold religious ideology, or what is known as religious commitment, look at the religious development of the curriculum as a central issue for them; they see an approach which advocates the range of sectarian affiliations as a typical political approach which aims to pose a challenge for the future generations of their community, and a betrayal of their heritage and their culture. For those who are concerned with the educational issue itself, especially those who have long service in teaching, they look to the curriculum from a national point of view rather than a religious one. They see the excesses of the new curricula but argue we cannot isolate religious teachers from the pressures of their culture and their environment which is generally controlled by tribal values.

THE CORE TEAM REFLECTS ON THEIR EXPERIENCE OF
THE FIRST IRFP WORKSHOP

Jawad Altamimi

The experience of working with CARA has both scientific and humanitarian dimensions. Taking part was a scientific experiment which is not completely new to me, but the humanitarian aspect of the experiment was an outstanding activity par excellence, although I came only once in Amman at the end of 2009. That was the first time I had ever met with a group of researchers and academics who were either non-Iraqi or Arabs. It is very important to see members of the human family – our Western colleagues – feel great moral responsibility towards a population living in a crisis point of the world and then gather in one place to help. If the language formed a barrier to the scientific aspect of the experiment, we were able to overcome this through the continued efforts of translation. There was a good feeling that contributed in breaking the psychological barriers which usually exist between the people belonging to different cultures when they meet in one place.

Joma'aAbd Allah Mutlaq

The best work environment is where the rigor in the times and methods are respected, coupled with the warmth of human relations and the propensity for good. They allow the researcher to get back to his humanity before getting him back to methodological tools. That was the impression left by the work in the CARA workshop.

In the Iraqi Imaginary there is a high sense of humanity about the organization Doctors without Borders, which has volunteered, since the early nineties, to help the Iraqis in the worst conditions of the blockade. This organization and similar organizations such as CARA, are trying to reassure and engage with the question marks that worry the minds of the majority. This anxiety is concerned with the meaning of Western modernity in its dealings with the Middle East, Muslims in particular. Big problems associated with this modernity are unnecessarily accumulated with the Muslim East, each time creating high barriers that need a deep understanding. Voluntary organizations, full of good sense and humanity, are needed in this deep spiritual emptiness experienced by human civilization. Iraq, getting out from womb of eternal wars, needs to re-connect with its history. For a country that invented the alphabet and the wheel and contributed to the first agricultural civilizations of Man, Iraq needs to get back to his meaningful existence.

In the five days of the IRFP workshop I attended the spirit of scientific research manifested itself, as all the participants focused on the meanings of this research with regard to methods and techniques, in combination with training in modern research methods and means. During all this no one acted like an expert or scientist, and there was a spirit of 'sacred' listening to the latest achievements of organized minds in a new field of expertise for us. Participants were moving in two circles: the first with regard to methodological experiences; the second with regard to the humanitarian aspect that allowed even for experts to learn from researchers or students, or their counterparts, in a manner that reflects fusion between science and ethics.

Dr. AbdAladheem Alsultany

Over a year and half ago I received an email from my old friend, Dr. Yahya Al-Kubaisi who I did not see since a long time, because of the circumstances that our country has passed through it. I doubly enjoyed the message: once on hearing from an old friend who invites me to join him in the team research work; and once because the project is worthy and provides the service of knowledge. So, I gave him my instant acceptance to participate in team work. After that I told him that I am not familiar with CARA the sponsors of the project, nor with their goals. However I trust the morals and knowledge of my friend who assured to me that it is a non-profit making Foundation which gives respectable support to scientific research in areas of tension and wars everywhere in the world.

The research trip was enjoyable. I have never tasted this pleasure before, because it is the first time that I have joined with a team to complete a research project. I used to carry out my research individually. This project gave me the opportunity to meet an impressive array of researchers in various humanitarian projects Pure Scientifics, academics who belong to a variety of human cultures, and widely experienced persons from all cultural dimensions.

The work is not empty of the difficulties which represent a real challenge: I'm from the city of Hilla, away from the capital Baghdad, about 100 km. The trip to Jordan to participate in the workshops in Amman obliged me to go to Baghdad more than one time for the purpose of obtaining a visa. Getting some information and sources was one of the difficulties that I faced. So I had to overcome this obstacle. This was achieved through my wide relations with friends, academics and researchers in different Iraqi and Arab universities to provide me with sources and addresses of some former colleagues who are dispersed everywhere in the world seeking for a safe place .

CONCLUSION

Academic Freedom in Iraqi School and Higher Education after 2003

In conclusion, social science research suffers in Iraq from very weak research methodology training and from an absence of a history of experimental field research in general. Weaknesses can be explained first because of the nature of the Iraqi Academia, as we have discussed earlier and secondly because of the lack of free access to information, and the presence of social, cultural, and political taboos.

The phase to carry out in-depth interviews with teachers was not easy: we had to choose four Iraqi provinces with different social characteristics for these interviews, and this was made difficult because of the problems of moving around in Iraq; and there is a climate of fear of having anything to do with the authorities which is still strongly present among Iraqis. There is a desire to have no involvement with the state, especially in matters which have sensitivity such as education. Therefore, we found a lot of teachers answering in a way that keeps them far from any 'classification', particularly in mixed ethnic and sectarian areas.

It is an obvious truth that Iraqi Higher Education has no autonomy or an independent academic will either before 2003 or after this date. The difference between before and after is a matter of quality and degree. The erosion of academic freedom in Iraqi universities continued to be the same, but the causes and threats changed. One can say that this erosion became deeper and wider after 2003, against what universities scholars expected and hoped from the Saddam regime downfall. The university system in Iraq was politicized under the control of military dictatorship before 2003 and under control of ideological (masked) dictatorships after 2003. In both regimes Higher Education is fully controlled by government. What I want to deal with here is determination of exact obstacles that stand before academic freedom in Iraq.

Universities produce knowledge, ideas and skills which nations today increasingly depend on, always with an abundance of intellectual diversity, and different perspectives in the ways of pursuing truth. The university is a core factory of ideas and thoughts, and a place where a variety of competing claims, avenues to truth can be explored and tested, free from heavy covers of ideologies and political interference. Universities in Iraq face critical problems. One of these problems is the absence of academic freedom, which may form the most dangerous factor to the darkness of the future of Higher Education in Iraq. Academic freedom is the freedom of scholars to search the truth (in teaching and research) upon the basis of independent thinking and open minds aside from fear, and the need for students to learn on the same basis.

Apart from political and financial freedom of universities from governmental control, I will focus upon the threats that badly influence the intellectual freedom of scholars in their teaching and research. Although political freedom and economical freedom are important incubators for intellectual freedom, intellectual freedom in Iraq is circumscribed by two aspects of violence; physical and psychological violence which former university scholars have faced inside or outside Iraq. There have been numerous assaults and cases of degradation. Assassination was sporadic and committed by different entities, most of them publicly unknown. In contrast, mental violence is more systematic and methodical, committed by known entities. Some of the perpetrators are governmental and others are connected with or oriented by governments. This latter kind of violence, which is the main cause of the absence of academic freedom, is dominant after a decrease in physical violence.

The mental or psychological violence could be represented in the following three representative aspects. Firstly, university curricula (particularly in humanities colleges) are old fashioned and oriented by religious, sectarian and sub-sectarian biases. Secondly, scholars are prevented from teaching subjects that are classified by administrative staff as sensitive according to the city that the university lies in. The truth should only have one face and one interpretation in this location, and should be reached by this particular way, which highly hampers the academic freedom in searching truth. Thirdly, most of the research in Iraqi universities is poor and below international standards because of administrative censorship (such as secret informers recently appointed in universities and colleges and surveillance cameras recently installed) according to limited religious, sectarian and sub-sectarian constraints and the party ideologies of administrative staff (who were appointed by their parties leaders) which form the governmental body. The international standards, topics, and methods are regarded by administrative staffs as subversive and hostile, so when the researchers' approach the prohibited triangle (sex, religion and politics) they face the accusation of being unbelievers and secular, a threat that makes academic freedom very vulnerable and even non-existent.

I conclude this chapter with some words of wisdom from the great British dramatist Shakespeare who lived in the 16th and early 17th centuries. I feel they can help us reflect on the conditions of research in Iraq and the role of CARA. The curriculum project team feels CARA exemplifies the candle in the Merchant of Venice where Shakespeare says: *'How far that little candle throws his beams! So shines a good deed in a naughty world!'* However with regard to the continued distinction made during our first IRFP meetings between policy and politics, and the philosophy that lies behind such a distinction, Shakespeare suggests through the mouth of Hamlet that *'There are more things in heaven and earth, Horatio than are dreamt of in your philosophy'*. The Iraqi people are frightened by research into their lives, and while this is understandable, Shakespeare also points out in Julius Caesar that *'Men at some time are masters of their fates: The fault, dear Brutus, is not in our stars but in ourselves, that we are underlings'*.

REFERENCES

Bourdieu, P., &Passeron, J-C. (1990). *Reproduction in Education, Culture and Society*. London: Sage.
Cromer, E.B. (1908). *Modern Egypt, Vol. 1*. London: The MacMillan Company.
Gramsci, A. *The Prison Notebooks*. New York: Columbia University Press.
Said, E. (1979). *Orientalism*. London: Vintage Books.
Said, E. (1996). *Representations of the Intellectual*. New York: Vintage Books.
UNESCO (2003).*Situation Analysis of Education in Iraq*, 2003. Paris.

ABDUL KAREEM AL-OBAIDI, ALI GHAZI KAMEES
AND TIM CORCORAN

5. EXPERIENCES OF INSUFFICIENCY

'Walking on a ledge in the dark'

INTRODUCTION

During 2009 CARA announced the Iraqi Research Fellowship Programme aiming to enhance research capacity among Iraqi academics. The IRFP allows scholars to conduct and disseminate advanced and modern research projects connecting these to Iraq's future academic development. This programme takes into consideration fostering and engaging the work of Iraqi academics in exile. One key expectation of the programme is for projects to have a positive impact on development of academia in Iraq in both the short and long term. It also facilitates international academic engagement fostering cooperation with Iraqi counterparts. This account is a reflection from a multidisciplinary team of researcher-practitioners facing these kinds of dilemmas the IRFP is intended to address. The context for the research involves paediatric training in Iraq and the potential extension of curriculum to involve psychosocial approaches to understanding human behaviour. Central to this account is an acknowledgement that in both research and practice, possibly one of the hardest decisions to make is not a choice of whether one possesses sufficient knowledge, but an acceptance that in not knowing we possibly find our way to get to where we want to be. This chapter discusses several challenges faced by an international research team as they embrace uncertainty together.

The Paediatric Psychosocial Training (PPT) project team includes Tim Corcoran as the Principal Investigator. Tim is an academic presently based in the UK whose background is in educational psychology. The Research Fellows and co-investigators are Abdul Kareem Al-Obaidi, an Iraqi scholar and medical doctor living in exile (USA), and Ali Ghazi and Mushriq Hussein, medical doctors and faculty members in a medical college in Baghdad. Due to circumstances beyond the control of the project Mushriq was unable to contribute to the writing of this chapter. What binds together the individual stories presented here is a dedication to the work each undertakes. All are practitioners in fields committed to servicing health-related needs of children and families (a child psychiatrist, a paediatric trainee and an educational psychologist).Having made these introductions the discussion moves to consider a subject known only too well to each team member, experiences of insufficiency. This disposition presents in their practice as health professionals, as researchers with varying degrees of proficiency and as

*H. Brunskell-Evans & M. Moore (Eds.), Reimagining Research for Reclaiming the Academy in Iraq:
Identities and Participation in Post-Conflict Enquiry: The Iraq Research Fellowship Programme, 65–77.*

contributors to the PPT project attempting to balance the complex demands of being researcher-practitioners. The key message to come from this reflection is an acknowledgement that uncertainty is an unavoidable outcome of being genuinely invested in research and practice. This should be used as a challenge to simultaneously reach for best practice but also strive to better prevailing conditions.

A BRIEF RATIONALE AND OUTLINE OF THE PROJECT

There is growing consensus among mental health professionals worldwide regarding the importance of complimentary and synchronized services involving clinical and community-based intervention (Inter-Agency Standing Committee, 2007).For children living in areas of armed conflict research has shown they are likely to experience increased mental health concerns as evidenced in studies undertaken in Jammu and Kashmir (de Jong & Van Ommeren, 2006), Mozambique (Richman, 1993), Sri Lanka (Somasundaram, 2004), the Gaza Strip (Thabet et al., 2002), Bosnia (Husain et al., 2008) and Lebanon (Karam et al., 2006).Mental health services supporting children in war-affected communities are subsequently broadening their focus from medically-driven curative approaches (i.e. clinical service responses) to incorporate more preventative, primary care level services (Jordans et al., 2009).In practice, these supports are encompassing more comprehensive, multimodal and multi-level intervention programmes (Stichick, 2001).

Presently, given the current absence of psychiatric and psychological resources in Iraq, responsibility for children's mental health intervention falls to paediatricians. This circumstance provided the impetus to the development of the project and will be discussed in further detail later in the chapter by the Iraqi members of the PPT. The overriding issue addressed by the research focuses on training currently delivered to paediatricians in Iraq questioning whether such preparation incorporates alternatives to clinically-based medical models of intervention. This concern is of particular importance given the evidential need for mental health services to work in multimodal ways and in multidisciplinary teams with other front-line social services (e.g. education).

The members of the PPT project collaboratively developed two main objectives for the study. These were:

i) To review current curriculum and educational practices involved in training paediatricians in child mental health with a focus on psychosocial approaches to health promotion, prevention and intervention; and

ii) Via questionnaires and interviews investigate the perspectives of paediatric trainers and trainees at a Baghdad University paediatric department regarding options for child mental health focussing on psychosocial approaches to health promotion, prevention and intervention.

Until greater capacity emerges with re-established professional groups e.g. Child Psychiatrists, Clinical and Educational Psychologists, School Counsellors and Social Work services, it is paediatricians who will shoulder responsibility for psychosocial care of children and families in the country. The PPT project aims are twofold: to build capacity within paediatric services with the intention of making a positive contribution to future service developments in Iraq.

PERSONAL JOURNEYS TO THE PPT TEAM

Kareem

One of the consequences of the 2003 war and USA led invasion of Iraq was the targeting of academics and medical doctors by insurgents, militias and other known and unknown gangs and criminal groups. As an established psychiatrist and scholar (running the only child psychiatric clinic in Baghdad), I found it difficult to leave my native country but threats of violence against my family made it impossible to remain. In the summer of 2006, my family and I fled from Iraq to Amman, Jordan. From there, I alone went to UK in the hope of finding a safe place for my family. Because of what seemed to be administrative inertia (i.e. British government inactiveness), attempts to resettle in the UK were not successful. During this period I was away from my family for more than a year. However, whilst I was in the UK I was introduced to the Council for Assisting Refugee Academics (CARA) and became involved with its programme. My contact and collaboration with CARA continued during the ensuing years whilst my family and I continued to search for a place to call home. This search took us on to Libya and Egypt, finally settling in the USA.

I saw my own personal involvement in the IRFP as an opportunity to contribute experience in the field of psychiatry, specifically issues concerning child mental health, and knowledge pertaining to people experiencing Post Traumatic Stress Disorder and other mental health issues related to the years of violence in Iraq. It is documented that there are increasing rates of psychosocial problems among children in Iraq (Al-Obaidi et al 2010a, Al-Jawadi and Abdul-Rhman 2007, Razoki et al., 2006). I have published a number of studies that address the impact of various forms of violence on Iraqi children and young people (Al-Obaidi 2011,2010, Al-Obaidi and Budosan 2011, Al-Obaidi et al 2010b, 2009, Al-Obaidi and Jeffrey 2009, Al-Obaidi and Piachaud 2007, Al-Obaidi and Scarth 2008). One priority in intervention efforts in Iraq is the promotion of physical and psychological recovery and the social reintegration of children. Prior to leaving Iraq I was a consultant and faculty member in a major paediatric hospital in Baghdad I recognised from clinical observations that the front-line of child mental health workers is made up of two main groups of professionals, school teachers and paediatricians.

From discussion with a number of teachers who I met during my practice and many of my Iraqi colleagues (e.g. paediatricians), I recognised that professional training for both groups has not placed an emphasis on understanding psychosocial issues affecting children (e.g. addressing issues of human capacity and social ecology).In the field of medicine, the stated aim of emphasising psychosocial awareness is not yet incorporated into general paediatric training (Nadder et al 2003, Shipley et al, 2005). From my knowledge of current practices in medical training in Iraq and via my professional clinical experience I knew there was no equivalent study in the health field in the country to date. I felt it was essential therefore to collaborate in a project aiming to build such a capacity in front-line medical staff (i.e. paediatricians) in Iraq.

Ali

I have seen many adults and children in my one and a half year medical residency presenting with what might seem to be, in the first instance, a physical complaint. But after careful history taking and conversation with the patients and/or their families I found that the actual cause of this suffering is more likely a mental issue (somewhere between psychological and social in origin), rather than the initial physical complaint. This circumstance pushed me to consider whether paediatricians have sufficient training in the field of psychosocial approaches and in doing so, whether our practice could be developed to more effectively assist Iraqi people.

This thinking led me to talk with one of the senior doctors, Dr. Ghazwan, who is a faculty member of the paediatric department of Al-Mustansyria University in Baghdad. When talking with Dr. Ghazwan about this subject he told me that a colleague of his, a child psychiatrist, was also interested in this topic and was thinking about conducting research around this issue.

After this talk with Dr. Ghazwan I was introduced to Kareem by email. He informed me of his concern that teachers and paediatricians were, in his opinion, the first line of professionals responding to children and their psychosocial issues. We agreed that these two groups needed to increase their awareness about how to deal with these issues and Dr Al-Obaidi asked me if I would be interested in joining him on the research project. With this invitation, the team began to emerge.

Tim

On a surprisingly warm spring morning in Sheffield I was at my desk working when a Skype request came up on the computer screen. Those who have used this means of communication will know that the receiver of the call can read the name of the person trying to contact them. It was a call from Roger Slee, Academic Co-ordinator of the IRFP. I knew Roger was in Amman, Jordan working with CARA on a programme I did not know many details about. Skype allows audio-visual contact and when I saw Roger he was with Kate Robertson, Deputy Executive Secretary of Caraway all had worked together a month earlier delivering a research methods workshop in Erbil, Iraq as part of a CARA sponsored project investigating the provision of educational services for disabled students.

After exchanging greetings I was told about one of the research projects that was under development at the workshop in Amman. Our conversation could not have lasted more than 15 minutes and by the end I had agreed to read this project's research proposal and later that morning, connect again via Skype with members of the project team. I had been informed by Roger and Kate that other research groups attending the workshop had posed a number of incisive questions regarding the methodological aspects of the project. In its initial conceptualisation the research was intended to evaluate the effectiveness of a cognitive-behavioural intervention for Iraqi school children psychologically affected by conflict in the country. Having hurriedly read the proposal I had an impression of the benevolent aims and objectives of the study but also experienced some unease with its clinically-driven experimental focus. Now, on reflection, it could be suggested that a strength of the IRFP is that it is open and responsive to critical evaluation and change.

Just prior to Skype call coming though my mind raced with questions: How was I going to be introduced to this research group? How might I position myself? What can feasibly be achieved in such a short exchange? Who am I to be afforded this incredible opportunity? I began my involvement with the team with significant experiences of insufficiency and, as this chapter recognises, not only was I not alone, they show no sign of waning.

PRACTICE

Kareem

In practice, the challenge of protecting and assuring optimal health is a moral and ethical issue and has been recognised in developed countries (Dujardin, 1994). However, Iraq at this time is not a well developed country. The consequences of more than three decades of war, violence and isolation from the wider world have had a great impact on the bases of scientific knowledge and practice, not only in the field of health education but in other humanitarian and social education and training as well. The effect of declining education options in Iraqi society has been compounded by a parallel deterioration of services in the health system. Economic prospects have also been adversely affected by the flight and displacement of millions of Iraqis leaving the country. This exodus includes experienced academics, scholars and medical professionals and has strongly influenced the wellbeing of Iraqis. This circumstance reduces knowledge developments and contributions to society and causes attrition of academic standards. In effect, the research base of universities in the country has collapsed.

Such events have impacted considerably on medical training and education programs in Iraq. In the field of medicine, the aim of emphasising psychosocial awareness is not yet incorporated into general paediatric training. Training institutes continue to use outdated programmes with a clear neglect of approaches divergent from the medical model. Education, at the level of universities, Higher Educational institutes and community-based programmes (e.g. public health settings), should incorporate multimodal and multidisciplinary ways of working. For example, there is a specific shortage of school and community engagement involving the few paediatricians and psychiatrists providing access to care for children in Iraq. This is especially relevant to the management of complex childhood psychosocial problems, including addressing the overall functioning of children with chronic illnesses and disabilities, as well as in the promotion of healthful lifestyle behaviours to prevent adult chronic diseases.

In practice, cross-disciplinary work in this field, though supported in more developed systems (e.g. in the US and Europe; see Belfer and Saxena, 2006), is not yet part of professional training programmes in Iraq. With developments in medicine and the contemporary Bio-Psycho-Social model in treatment and research approaches, all treatment has to involve a negotiation with the patient, where best evidence is shared. Because these are human encounters, there will always be some uncertainty which we must learn to live with as professionals. We have a need to be able to say 'I do not know', a practice that is not well appreciated presently in Iraq.

Studies which will help to re-instate the research base for caring services in Iraq are urgently required. In doing so, evidence–based teaching and service provision can be built into the recovering intellectual life of Iraq to prevent the adoption of random ill-focussed interventions. It is clear that health and related social service professionals support the dictum 'Do no harm'. And yet, whatever oath we swear to there is no ideal best practice. With time medicine and other sciences are always changing and evolving and what was acceptable 30 years ago is almost certainly superseded now. Societies need up-to-date validated information to give the best current practices to our patients. This is the purpose of the research project being described here. Finally, we should substitute what is acceptable for what is best and this is always a negotiation between doctor and patient/family, community traditions and cultures as essential aspects for intervention should also be recognised.

Ali

Health care providers like physicians face many uncertainties in our decisions in practice because we are faced with cases where we think the diagnosis is very clear and straight forward. Then, after a concentrated history taking (discussion with the patient and/or their relatives), we find ourselves in a whole new place that is far away from the original understanding. For example, on occasion patients present with abdominal pain or chest pain and we think that their complaint is physical – as we always do. But after a few questions posed to the family we find out that they have been witness to other problems (e.g. relationship difficulties between parents).On other occasions a parent came to us crying and saying 'Please help my child he is in pain'. After the examination we found that the child has nothing evidently wrong but the parent on this occasion had lost a previous child in an explosion so he started to think that the child is having a problem even when he is healthy.

As health professionals we are perpetually trying to improve our practice in one way or another but because in the field of health care there are only few fixed facts about what is good and what is detrimental for the patient, in many occasions we end up asking ourselves: Is what I am doing is really the best approach for my patient? And if not, what is? We can continue: What if there are other approaches that I am not aware of that can inform a better method of treatment? And who decides what is better from those two approaches? Is it me (i.e. the practitioner) who is responsible to make this decision? This can lead to a struggle between what health professionals have been taught and what we think, based on our clinical experience, might be better.

Currently paediatric training in Iraq does not place great emphasis, if any, on the education of paediatric trainees in psychosocial issues or approaches. Most of the focus is on physical issues and their consequences because this is standard knowledge when learning clinical sciences such as paediatrics and medicine. This problem, I have found, creates a sense of insufficiency when facing these aspects in clinical practice.

Tim

I have been fortunate in my life not to have experienced firsthand the kinds of conditions Kareem and Ali know only too well. As someone who has practiced as a psychologist for over 10 years, my professional engagements with people have occurred mostly in Australia, in the main a safe and stable society. For most of this time I worked as an Educational Psychologist counselling children and their families (Corcoran, 2007). Whilst the issues being presented then were vastly different from those affecting people in Iraq now, as a practitioner I too have experienced times of doubt and uncertainty regarding my input as a mental health professional. For example, who would not question the quality of one's own professional contribution in the face of another human being's ongoing and persistent psychological distress? Particularly as new practitioners, we enter our professional lives often having been trained to 'fix' such problems, as would a mechanic when asked to service your car. With the benefit of hindsight I have affirmed what I thought I knew as an undergraduate student – people are not machines and never did I feel it necessary to wear overalls to work.

RESEARCH

Kareem

CARA has longstanding and excellent record for social and financial support of refugee academics. Since 2006, the charity has responded to the campaign of assassination and kidnapping targeting Iraq's academics. CARA does so via programmes involving Iraqi scholars and academics still living and working in the country and for those who have sought a life outside the country. CARA seeks to ensure that academics preserve their skills and expertise and assists them in finding ways to contribute to reconstruction efforts in Iraq.

The IFRP is one such activity of CARA. This programme aims to enhance research capacity among exiled Iraqi academics as well as supporting colleagues still living in Iraq. To personally contribute to the IRFP and the short and long term development of the academy in Iraq, I thought that involving young academics like

Drs Ali and Mushriq would be a suitable endeavour. Both will learn from this experience while they are professionally active and will gain necessary knowledge to conduct modern research projects. Knowledge of both quantitative and qualitative research models is important. However, a qualitative research project is unique for medical research in Iraq due to a number of obstacles facing researchers including a lack of training in conducting such research, in addition to other factors like shortage of resources and general difficulties due to the state of insecurity. There is an issue of Iraqi confidence in the home-based academy at this time, for issues of contemporary concern can only be truly appreciated by those with experience on-the-ground living in the country. Surely this is why we have insisted on an Iraqi base for the research. Drs Ali and Mushriq will form the core of our team and I see that they may lead, in near future, further research work, acting as role models for other trainees in the field.

As members of a multidisciplinary research team who are living in different countries (USA, UK and Iraq), we may expect some communication barriers like setting up team meetings, travel and visa issues. However, with a clear aim for the project, our interest and commitment to assist our society, moreover the availability of communication technology will give us the incentive to overcome such difficulties.

I think there is an artificial division between academic and researcher. A good academic must be aware of and involved in research so that their teaching and practice can be developed and not static. As such, our research focus is on exploring with and not prescribing or dictating certain views to trainers/trainees on psychosocial issues. We do not know if attitudes need changing until we have asked the appropriate questions and gathered the relevant information. However, my Iraqi colleagues and I have made some assumptions based on our experiences. If the trainers reflexively know, then we should have information about where change is required. The purpose of recruiting trainee potential academics is to teach skills which we have acquired in the research area, such as information gathering and techniques of analysis.

The issue of the ethical approval is one I raised a long time ago in my home country and whilst the audience appreciated the concern nothing further was implemented. I would have been more comfortable with the availability for Iraqi ethics approval (as opposed to only UK approval) for our project, as I think this would have allowed a stronger Iraqi ownership of the project. However, currently there are no legally empowered research ethical committees in the universities in Iraq. Research ethical committees are another potential area of development and should be encouraged, legislated and endorsed, especially at Higher Educational and research institutes in Iraq.

Ali

I have known Mushriq since I began my days of residency in the child central teaching hospital in Baghdad. While we were working in the ward we discovered that we both share an interest in the social impact of disease but we did not have any psychological or psychiatric expert advice regarding our inquiry. From our willingness to explore our interests we met Kareem. The contact between Mushriq, Kareem and I enabled reciprocal relationships to develop. In one way, Kareem was able to enter in to the field of paediatric training regarding its curriculum and courses. In another, the relationship has enabled us to consider what a psychiatrist thinks regarding psychosocial approaches in paediatric and/or medical training.

The aim of our project is to consider whether there is a perceived need for paediatricians to learn about psychosocial approaches. And if there is support for our suggestion, to what extent does this kind of training need to be included in current paediatric curriculum? Many people, most of them our colleagues, asked us about the intentions of CARA in a research project like this, as it is common to doubt western or foreign intervention in Iraq. Many people saw CARA's motives as insufficient. The same people asked us why we cared to address an issue like this. Some people thought that we are working for a personal benefit we will receive from this research and others said that we are undertaking research for a foreign person with a hidden agenda.

Presently in Iraq training and research mostly assumes quantitative methods so to do qualitative research is a new concept for us and our colleagues in the paediatric department. For Mushriq and I to engage in this project, we needed to explore how to deal with qualitative data and different ways to analyze it. The method by which we are going to gather information in our research depends on two modes: initial surveys and then interviews to be conducted after the initial survey is done. Many of our colleagues are reluctant to participate in the interview if it will involve any voice recording as this is the common suspicion about any research or programme that is supported by western organisations.

Tim

As noted above in my recollection of initial contact with the earlier version of this project, upon reading the proposal I was concerned with the clinically-driven experimental focus of the research. The empirical research I have conducted to date has been qualitative in nature focussing on language use as a form of social practice e.g. discourse used to describe individuals under State sanction (e.g. school exclusion or adult incarceration; see Corcoran, 2003, 2005).I was interested in contributing to the revisioning of the project as I could see an important contribution being made from changes to its aims and objectives. A primary goal of the IRFP is to build research capacity within the academy in Iraq. By undertaking a qualitative research project the team is actively pursuing this goal in a medical context. Following this, there is a more philosophically oriented prospect that interests me which has to do with opening deliberations to ways in which we (health professionals and the people they consult) envisage our world (Corcoran, 2009).This leads to directly questioning ontological issues which, too often in my opinion, are insufficient in medical (e.g. psychiatry or paediatrics) and social science (e.g. psychology) research via a penchant for quantitative applications.

RESEARCHER-PRACTITIONER

Kareem

It is very challenging to be committed to a project such as ours. It is anticipated that the research will take two years to complete, with a team geographically separated and, at times, holding different visions. For me, it is an essential project into which I have invested considerable thought and time. I am committed to seeing it accomplish its goals. However, I have to be realistic in my thinking about the outcomes, taking in consideration the many real-life difficulties including sparing time for the project, work, family and several other commitments. I also hold major concerns regarding the safety of our team members in Baghdad with the current security situation in Iraq and its unpredictable consequences. In gathering data, pursuing people to participate and responding to the research survey, they are taking on a worthwhile but heavy task. In addition, there are obstacles which I and my Iraqi colleagues face in terms of travelling, which include securing visas to attend research team meetings outside Iraq.

I understand from my experience and knowledge in the field of mental health, the impact of social stigma and via my commitment to this work, its potential relationship to one's health and/or academic status. In Iraq many might see work with psychosocial issues as being unnecessary in the face of huge shortages in other important areas of daily living, e.g. security, food and electricity. It is challenging for our team to raise the importance of psychological wellbeing of people who face such urgent day to day needs. It is said that 'there is no health without mental health'(WHO, 1948). In spite of some opposition to this I believe this standard applies as much to Iraq as it does to the UK or any other society. I think that in a small yet potentially significant way this project will support this proposition in its effect on future attitudes to the teaching of such issues in academic training programmes in Iraq.

Ali

One of the greater challenges we face during the conduct of our research is to balance our schedules between full time jobs and the research. This is because Mushriq and I are resident doctors spending most of our days in the hospital doing our shifts. In the spare time that we have we usually spend it reading and preparing for the exams or reading just to improve ourselves and our practice. More often than not we do not have any spare time at all. But for this research to succeed we have to create time. It is very difficult for us to allocate time for the research and even after doing so we end up not progressing with our agreed schedule because we are exhausted from our jobs and have no energy left to go and work on the research. It is therefore easy to conclude that not progressing with the research can cause frustration and feelings of guilt because we feel that we are not committed to our deadlines and to our colleagues.

On the other hand, frustration of one team member can be managed or healed by other team members and here appears another problem experienced from being involved in this project – being separated and so far away from each other. If any one of the team members needs an illustration, clarification or even a hand on the shoulder to tell him that he did a good job, he has to wait for it!!!And because electronic accessibility and internet services are not the same in every country, it is not always easy for the team members to communicate.

In Iraq the people in general tend to hide or suppress their own and their family's psychological, social and mental problems because it is thought as stigmatising. Only very few people who have problems decide to go and seek specialist care. For this reason few people choose to access mental health care because it is felt unneeded by the community. That is why a research like ours, asking about psychosocial approaches, may be regarded as unneeded by both the patient and the doctor and for this reason research like ours is important because only very few care about this field and want to make changes in it.

Tim

From my days as an undergraduate psychology student I knew two things: I wanted to go on to undertake detailed research at a doctoral-level but I also wanted to go out in to a world beyond academia to practice my chosen discipline. From very early on in my professional life the model I envisaged was of being a researcher-practitioner. To be either alone would be, for me, insufficient. As the record shows, having graduated from university, my first job as a psychologist was at the prison on the outskirts of the town I lived in. Following two years working there I then worked for eight years as the District Psychologist for government pre-school to Year 12 schools in the region. Both roles enabled my thinking particularly regarding how psychological theories contribute to constructing knowledge of people and the world we inhabit. And today, now that my time is dedicated to academia, I still remain connected to practice volunteering as a Counsellor at my University's Counselling Service.

One aspect of the initial project that grabbed my attention was the fact that Kareem, Ali and Mushriq are practitioners dedicated to improving children's mental health in their country. It was also apparent that via their involvement in the IRFP they each had a vested interest in making a positive contribution to rebuilding the academy in Iraq. As we discussed potential options for reconfiguring the proposal it quickly became apparent that the project could have a greater and lasting effect if it were to research the training of future practitioners. Once we decided to reconceptualise the research in this way, the PPT was earnestly underway. Whilst there are distinct differences within our team (e.g. disciplinary background, practice experience, research expertise, etc.), it is each member's commitment to engaging as a researcher-practitioner that indubitably binds us together.

CONCLUSION

The trajectory of the PPT project has been unpredictable, starting off as an evaluative research project involving a school-based cognitive-behavioural intervention to its present incarnation as a Higher Education-based paediatric training review. The members of the team hope that from having read this account the reader will have sufficient understanding of several challenges faced by the project to date. Undertaking research is often not a simple endeavour and this is certainly the case when the project involves an international team and circumstance like that presently affecting Iraq. In this account the team members specifically wanted to draw attention to the three areas highlighted – practice, research and the researcher-practitioner – for it was in these areas the team share experiences of insufficiency, commitment and motivation. Whilst these drive the PPT there is also a clear purpose in being part of the IRFP and the ensuing opportunity to contribute to rebuilding Higher Education in the country. The IRFP will not by itself accomplish this task for the challenge is considerable. But via the achievement of short and long-term goals, such as the ones outlined here and more broadly in this volume, efforts are being realised which simultaneously develop self-sufficiency and collectively add to reclamation of the academy in Iraq.

REFERENCES

Al-Obaidi, A.K. (2011) Iraq: Children and Adolescents' Mental Health under Continuous Turmoil, *International Psychiatry,8*(1), 5–6.

Al-Obaidi, A.K. (2010) Iraqi psychiatrist in exile helping distressed Iraqi refugee children in Egypt in non-clinical settings. *Journal of the Canadian Academy of Child and Adolescent Psychiatry.* Volume *19*,2, 72–73.

Al-Obaidi, A.K., and Budosan B. (2011) Mainstreaming Educational Opportunities for Physically and Mentally Disabled Children Youth in Iraq. *Advances in School Mental Health Promotion.* Volume *4*(1), 35–43.

Al-Obaidi, A.K., Scarth, L., and Dwivedi, K.N., (2010a) Mental disorder in children attending child psychiatric clinic at the general paediatric hospital in Baghdad. *The International Journal of Mental Health Promotion.* Volume *12*(3), 24–30.

Al-Obaidi, A.K., Budosan, B., and Jeffery, L., (2010b) Child and adolescent mental health in Iraq: current situation and scope for promotion of child and adolescent mental health policy. *Intervention,* Volume *8*(1), 40–51.

Al-Obaidi, A.K., and Jeffrey, L.R. (2009) Iraq; In Malley-Morrison, K. (Ed.), *State violence and the right to peace: An international survey of the views of ordinary people.* Praeger Security International, CA, USA; 147–159.

Al-Obaidi , A.K., Jeffrey, L.R., Scarth, L., and Albadawi, G. (2009) Iraqi Children Rights: Build a system under fire. *Medicine, Conflict & Survival, 25*(2), 145–162.

AlObiadi, A.K., and Piachaud, J., (2007) While adults battle, children suffer: Future problems for Iraq. *Journal of Royal Society of Medicine, 100*, 394–395.

Al-Obaidi , A.K.,Scarth, L., (2008) *Children without protection, the innocent victims in Iraq.* IACAPAP Bulletin; April 2008, issue xix, *3–4.*

Al-Jawadi, A.A., and Abdul-Rhman, S. (2007) *Prevalence of childhood and early adolescence mental disorders among children attending primary health care centers in Mosul, Iraq: a cross-sectional study.* BMC Public Health. Open Access Article. Available from: http://www.biomedcentral.com/ 1471-2458/7/274.

Belfer, M.L., and Saxena, S. (2006) WHO Child Atlas Project. *Lancet, 367*, 551–552.

Corcoran, T. (2009) Second Nature. *British Journal of Social Psychology, 48*(2), 375–388.

Corcoran, T. (2007) Counselling in a discursive world. *International Journal for the Advancement of Counselling, 29*(2), 111–122.

Corcoran, T. (2005).Legislative practice as discursive action. *International Journal for the Semiotics of Law,18*(3/4), 263–268.

Corcoran, T. (2003) Constructing dialogic relationships: School legislation and the Principal's gamble. *Australia & New Zealand Journal of Law & Education, 8*(2), 97–109.

de Jong, J.T., and Van Ommeren, M. (2006) Mental health services in a multicultural society: interculturalization and its quality surveillance. *Transcultural Psychiatry, 42*, 437–456.

Dujardin, B. (1994) Health and Human Rights: The challenge for developing countries. *Social* Vol. 39(9), 1261–1274.

Husain, S.A., Allwood, M.A., and Bell, D.J. (2008) The relationship between PTSD symptoms and attention problems in children exposed to the Bosnian war. *Journal of Emotional and Behavioural Disorders, 16*(1), 52–62.

Inter-Agency Standing Committee (2007) *Inter-Agency Standing Committee Guidelines on Mental Health and Psychosocial Support in Emergency Settings.* Geneva: ISAC.

Jordans, M.J.D., Tol, W.A., Komporoe, I.H., and de Jong, J.T. (2009) Systematic review of evidence and treatment approaches: psychosocial and mental health care for children in war. *Child and Adolescent Mental Health, 14*(1), 2–14.

Karam, E.G., Mneimneh, Z.N., Karam, A.N., Fayyad, J.A., Nasser, S.C., Chatterji, S., and Kessler, R.C. (2006) Prevalence and treatment of mental disorders in Lebanon: a national epidemiological survey. *Lancet, 367*, 1000–1006.

Nader, P R., Broyles, S L., Brennan, J, and Taras, H., (2003) Two National Surveys on Pediatric Training and Activities in School Health: 1991 and 2001. *Pediatrics, 111*, 730–734.DOI: 10.1542/peds.111.4.730.

Razoki, A.H., Taha, I.K., Taib, N.I., Sadik, S., and Al Gasseer, N. (2006) Mental health of Iraqi children. *Lancet, 368*, 838–839.

Richman, N. (1993) Annotation: Children in situations of political violence. *Journal of Child Psychology and Psychiatry, 34*, 1286–1302.

Shipley, L J., Stelzner, S M., Zenni, E A., Hargunani, D., O'Keefe, J., Miller, C., Alverson, B., and Swigonski, N., (2005) Teaching Community Pediatrics to Pediatric Residents: Strategic Approaches and Successful Models for Education in Community Health and Child Advocacy. *Pediatrics, 115*, 1150–1157.

Somasundaram, D. (2004) Short and long-term effects of the victims of terror in Sri Lanka. *Journal of Aggression, Maltreatment and Trauma, 9*, 215–228.

Stichick, T. (2001) The psychosocial impact of armed conflict on children: Rethinking traditional paradigms in research and intervention. *Child and Adolescent Psychiatry Clinics of North America, 10*, 797–814.

Thabet, A.A., Abed, Y., Vostanis, P., de Jong, J., and Komproe, I.H., (2002) Emotional problems in Palestinian children living in a war zone: A cross-sectional study. *Lancet, 359*(9320), 1801–1804.

WHO (1948) *.Report of the Interim Commission to the first World Health Assembly.* Official records of the World Health Organization No.9. Available at:http://whqlibdoc.who.int/hist/official_records/9e.pdf.

ALAA MUSA KHUTTAR, KARIM AL-JEBOURY AND KEVIN
MCDONALD

6. MOBILE PHONE TECHNOLOGIES AND DIABETES: A PROJECT FOR SELF-MANAGEMENT AND EDUCATION

INTRODUCTION

One area of CARA's attempt to support academics outside of Iraq while working to respond to urgent challenges facing the country has been in the area of health. This chapter explores key dimensions of an attempt to build a research and intervention project through harnessing mobile health technologies to respond to the urgent health imperative of diabetes. Perhaps more than other areas, this project highlights both the possibilities but also the challenges faced in our attempt to build new types of research intervention in a context shaped by the legacy and ongoing realities of war.

WAR, HEALTH AND MEDICAL SERVICES

One of the key factors shaping the context in which our research intervention developed is the legacy of war and sanctions. The sanctions period of the 1990s not only targeted military technologies, it had the effect of isolating universities from their international networks and disciplines, while drastically reducing the availability of medical equipment and the possibilities for medical training. This meant that even before the war of 2003, Iraq's medical infrastructure was profoundly weakened. The declining capacity of the public medical system was evident in the expansion of various forms of private health provision, not as part of an attempt to respond to the realities of the country but often driven by those who had funds to pay for health services. The context of sanctions and shortages also saw the growth of a significant black market for medical supplies and technologies.

The war and state of chronic violence and insecurity that followed highlight key dimensions of contemporary armed conflict, in particular in terms of casualties and impact of war on the wider society. In the First World conflict largely took place in zones that were isolated from civilian life, with over 95% of those killed being military personnel, and less than 5% of deaths being civilians. In the Second World War we see a decisive change, as protagonists set out to target cities and civil infrastructure, leading to some 50% of those killed being civilians. By the wars of the 1990s the pattern of the First World War was effectively reversed, with 90% of

H. Brunskell-Evans & M. Moore (Eds.), Reimagining Research for Reclaiming the Academy in Iraq:
Identities and Participation in Post-Conflict Enquiry: The Iraq Research Fellowship Programme, 79–87.
© *2012 Sense Publishers. All rights reserved.*

those killed being non-military personnel (Chesterman 2001: 2). The war that began in Iraq in 2003 involves both continuity and change in this pattern. The massive majority of deaths due to war have been civilians, but at the same time, targeting both physical and organizational infrastructure became one of the principal ways that war was prosecuted, while the phase of the war following invasion saw massacres, explosions in urban environments, and military occupation. This, combined with the use of weapons using depleted uranium and strategies aiming at the obliteration of human habitation as evident in the destruction of Fallujah in 2004, means that war produced social, environmental as well as governmental collapse, evident in water shortages and the extent of pollution of drinking water, the development of smuggling and illegal markets in medical supplies, often stolen from hospitals and sold on the streets. These all directly translate into health outcomes, evident in widespread trauma and significant increase in mental illness, as well as increasing rates of malnutrition, anemia, death at childbirth, cancers and so on (UNFPA, 2007, 87–91).

While the war generated a new set of health problems, it also brought about a drastic degradation of the already weakened health system, with many medical personnel being targeted and killed by militias and armed groups. This violence and the resulting sense of being part of a profession that was being systematically targeted combined with the collapse of careers and in many cases the impossibility of simply working, and led to a significant exodus of doctors and other medical personnel from the country at a time when new and urgent health problems were becoming more and more pressing. Among these diabetes has emerged as particularly urgent.

THE CHALLENGE OF DIABETES

Diabetes is a non-communicable disease involving chronically high levels of blood sugar (glucose) in the body, with consequences that can affect all major body organs. Diabetes mellitus or Type 2 Diabetes (formerly often referred to as 'adult onset' diabetes) is largely irreversible, and has a particularly high incidence in Iraq, and involves very significant consequences if it not appropriately managed. These include heart disease, nerve disorders, peripheral arterial disease leading to loss of limbs, and eye disorders such as glaucoma and cataracts leading to blindness, as well as significant complications in pregnancy and childbirth (for background on diabetes in Iraq, see WHO 2007).At one level the challenge of diabetes involves prevention and health education, because the incidence of this disease can be significantly reduced through healthy lifestyle. But in many cases this is extremely difficult, and for the large section of the Iraqi population currently experiencing diabetes, the challenge is to develop ways of managing the disease so that serious health complications do not develop. This is an extraordinarily difficult challenge in contemporary Iraq given its fractured health service, meaning often diabetes sufferers encounter late diagnosis and poor management by health services.

All this leads to a situation where diabetes is ranked at the fifth cause of early mortality in Iraq today. Because of its chronic nature, and the severe consequences of complications, the successful management of diabetes is critical to patient wellbeing. This includes factors such as diet and exercise, as well as regular monitoring of blood sugar levels to ensure that these are within a safe range. This process requires a significant level of support and interaction between the patient and health service providers, while the situation in Iraq means that this is often extremely difficult to achieve. It is this failure of management of the disease that is at the heart of the high mortality rate associated with diabetes in Iraq, and this was the principal challenge that our project set out to respond to.

OUR PROJECT

Our project sets out to address the challenge of diabetes in Iraq through developing a series of initiatives using mobile phones as a platform for health intervention. The aim is to use mobile phones to both enhance self-management of the disease and as a platform for health education. Together these goals are part of what has come to be known over recent years as 'm-health', a series of innovations that opens out important possibilities in countries such as Iraq, where significant difficulties in accessing medical services as a result of the degraded state of the health system combine with major difficulties associated with travel because of security problems. In this context, the mobile phone becomes an important communication and intervention tool, with the World Bank estimating in 2011that mobile phone penetration had reached 77% of the Iraqi population (Hamdan 2011).

The project was initiated by Professor Robert Istepanian of the University of Kingston in London, who brought together an interdisciplinary research team made up of a diabetologist, a software engineer, and a data system designer, together with key support being offered by medical practitioners and scholars in the United Kingdom. The team joined scholars who had left Iraq with scholars working in the country, while linking these into international support networks, and also entering into collaboration with a major provider of mobile phone services in Iraq.

The project began work in 2008, and has been working to develop a system that will allow individuals who have diabetes to monitor their blood sugar levels, and with the help of a mobile phone, to upload this data to health services. The aim of the project has been to develop simple systems that will facilitate the self-management of diabetes, while at the same time developing a system that can be used as a means of health promotion. Much of the early work of the project has focused on technical issues, such as developing protocols that will allow accurate measurement of blood sugar levels, and the construction of software that will allow this data to be easily transferred from a glucometer to the mobile phone, and then to be uploaded to a central server. One of the aims of the project has been to eventually develop technology that can be used among poorer and isolated social groups, so we have been aiming at developing a system based on low cost mobile phones, as opposed to high-end products. This has meant that the technical development has proceeded using Java as the basis of a Diabetes Management System, this being chosen on the basis that it allows simple phones to be used, while also being open to higher end technologies. The aim of the Management

System is to develop an easily accessed and understandable personalised web-based profile, where both medical staff and users of the system can monitor key data around the management of their condition.

The technical dimensions of this project have been at the heart of its first period, and these have confronted us with the key aspects of contemporary Iraq: how to link a glucometer to a mobile phone; how to transmit data; how to ensure that this is securely and reliably linked to an individual patient profile; how to ensure that the profile thus created is both secure yet also easily accessed by medical practitioners and patients. Our team is a collaboration of researchers in several cities: Basra, Baghdad, Amman and London, and the difficulties of travel and even reliable email communication have proved a constant challenge to overcome. The availability of basic technical infrastructure has also been a challenge, in particular the need to access a secure server in order to store confidential personal health data, meaning that the server must be physically located in a way that guarantees security of its data. While colleagues in many countries can presume that such infrastructure will be available, this has not been the case in Iraq. In the end a server had to be brought to Iraq from the United Kingdom via Amman, as part of the baggage of team members while travelling. The organizational and technical support infrastructure that in many countries exists to support research is generally not available in Iraq. In responding to this challenge, support from the Medical School at Basra University has been of decisive importance.

RESEARCH DESIGN AND ETHICS

After two-years of work that has largely focused on technical challenges, we are at the point of setting up a pilot project. Reaching this point has involved work on the parameters and infrastructures necessary for a mobile platform for diabetes management that will work within the technical constraints that we encounter in Iraq. This has involved overcoming not only technical issues. One of our greatest challenges has been build a research team. In part this has involved dealing with communications issues. But at a more substantial level, the team we have been building brings together medical researchers together with software and computer engineers, and there is very little experience within Iraq of such cross disciplinary research teams.

These different disciplines have quite different ways of approaching problems, one focusing on technical processes, the other on patient-medical practitioner interactions. Approaches to research and research design tend to be quite different within these disciplines, with the technical disciplines tending to focus on building a model and implementing it as the research method, while much medical research is framed in terms of population-based studies, in particular the use of 'double-blind' studies that typically set out to test a product or procedure among two groups, where neither research participants nor the researcher knows which is the 'test' group and which is the 'control' group. As a team we have had to build a research strategy that will generate robust data, even at the level of a small pilot study, and this has been a major challenge for us.

This has been mirrored by the challenge of research ethics. Generally this is not an issue in laboratory-based technology disciplines, but is a key question when people are involved as research participants. This is a key dimension of our study, since we are asking people to trial a method of managing a serious health problem. We need to be sure that they understand the implications of what is involved, and we have to be sure that participants understand that they are part of a research study, not a new form of health management. It is critically important that we do not, for example, inadvertently lead research participants to believe that since their health data is being uploaded to a server they are absolved from the responsibility of managing their condition. It is possible they might believe that the researchers are taking on a role of clinical responsibility. These are all key dimensions to the ethical design of this study.

In order to respond to these challenges, we have drawn upon British Medical Association research ethics material, and received important support from project mentors in the United Kingdom. This support was critical in thinking through issues of research ethics, and even at a more basic level, in designing the study's Plain Language Statement and Consent Form. The design of these documents plays a key role in the ways participants understand research, its potential risks, and the fact that at any point they can withdraw from the study. These are very important issues in Iraq, in particular in a context where there may be very different levels of education or social status between researchers and research participants. We must be sure that research participants fully understand what they are consenting to become involved in, and that they are fully aware that they are free to withdraw at any time. Designing research in this way is not easy. In many countries researchers can rely not only upon the mentoring of experienced colleagues, but also on a significant body of research infrastructure, ranging from published work on research ethics to the role of professional associations and national statements on human research ethics. As it has developed, our study has underlined the critical importance of strengthening the research ethics infrastructure in Iraqi universities. This is as a key dimension to rebuilding the research capacity of the country, and the international research networks supported by CARA have played a real role in this, not only in terms of our project, but more widely through the impact that our grappling with these questions has had in our respective universities. Without doubt, this remains a critical challenge for the future of research in Iraq.

REGIONAL PERSPECTIVES

Our project has had important interest and support in the Middle East and North Africa (MENA) region, with two 'regional Round Table s' being organized to explore more general strategies around developing mobile platforms for diabetes management. These Round Tables brought together researchers, public health officials and representatives from phone companies, the countries involved being Iraq, Jordan, Egypt and Palestine, together with the United Kingdom. Important expressions of interest came from several other countries, while participation was limited as a result of visa and travel problems.

There is an emerging consensus that Type 2 Diabetes is at the centre of an emerging public health crisis in the MENA region, with a recent estimate suggesting that 7.7% of the adult population of the region (26 million people) were suffering from Diabetes in 2010, this figure expected to double by 2030.Current estimates suggest that some 14% of the total health care budget in the MENA region is spent on diabetes and diabetes-related health complications. This concern is reflected more globally in the United Nations Resolution 61/225 on Diabetes of 20 December 2006, while the World Economic Forum identifies diabetes as a global risk threatening the achievement of the Millennium Development Goals. As a result, there is a very strong awareness throughout the MENA region of the challenge posed by Diabetes prevention and management, and a very clear commitment to transformative research (see MENA Diabetes Leadership Forum 2010).Our project is one of the few exploring the potential role of mobile technologies in the prevention and management of the disease, and the two CARA Round Tables formulated the outlines of a strategy to develop an m-health network in the MENA region, supported by scholars and institutions in the United Kingdom. The aim of the network is to strengthen research links and practice across the region, with a particular emphasis on research that has an impact at the level of health policy.

These two Round Tables were important opportunities to consider medical and health education more broadly in the MENA region, highlighting the importance of integrating m-health into the curriculum, and in the future looking to the development of post-graduate education in the area of m-health. The area of curriculum development has been a small, but significant outcome of our project, which has led to several discussions around the importance of integrating health promotion and health education in the medial curriculum, and to exploring ways this might be linked with m-health. Our project has also highlighted the crucial importance of collaboration between different health professionals in the area of diabetes care, and has noted that strategies to support patient self-management need to be strengthened in the medical curriculum. In cases such as diabetes, effective patient self-management is critical to long term health outcomes, but the medical curriculum may not attach sufficient important to understanding the experience of illness, and the ways that people relate to their bodies when experiencing illness in general, and diabetes in particular. Sometimes, from a medical perspective, this is seen simply as whether the patient follows the instructions of the doctor. However the challenge of supporting patient self-management goes beyond 'compliance' with a doctor's instructions, we are faced with the need to understand complex embodied experience and the embodied meanings of health and illness, perhaps in particular in relation to chronic health problems such as diabetes. Integrating these dimensions is essential if we are to successfully develop an m-health intervention. The aim is not to reproduce relationships of dependence, but to support new forms of autonomy and responsibility. It is possible that the relationship and familiarity people have with their mobile phone can be a real asset in the development of m-health interventions, and this will be an important area for us to understand in the pilot project.

The Round Tables also signalled the importance of new types of forums bringing together medical professionals, public health officials, political leaders and civil society organizations. This highlighted that the increasing incidence of diabetes is not simply a medical challenge, but a social and cultural problem. Rather than simply a technical problem that can be solved by the delivery of services through the Ministry of Health, successful health strategies include what the Round Table called 'social mobilization', an engagement with contemporary culture, and a strengthening of civil society. This remains a major challenge in a country where the legacies of violence and war still remain very much part a part of day-to-day experience.

THE CHALLENGE OF INTEGRATING SOCIAL AND CULTURAL DIMENSIONS

One theme that emerged strongly in the Round Tables when we presented our research was the need to integrate the social and cultural dimensions. This ranges from sensitivity to the power relations between medical practitioners and potential research participants or the importance of designing technologies that facilitate independence as opposed to creating new types of dependency, to the need to understand much more deeply the social processes involved in both ill-health and the successful promotion of wellness. M-health is not simply a matter of technologies and systems, it also involves understanding the role mobile technologies and the forms of communication they sustain play in the lives of Iraqis today. The Round Tables highlighted, for example, the importance of contemporary 'upload culture', and the need to find ways of integrating social media into health promotion and health delivery.

We have seen over the past year the way communications technologies and social media have revolutionised politics in the MENA region, and our small project seeks to draw on such social and cultural change. While computing and telecommunications technologies and systems are crucial, successful m-health interventions also need to respond to the ways people use mobile communications. In particular such interventions need to understand the ways in which contemporary mobile communications increase people's autonomy, and our research needs to succeed in integrating these dimensions into the system we develop. The social and cultural dimensions of mobile communications technologies were strongly emphasised at the Round Tables, participants emphasising the importance of broadening out our research team to include social scientist who would play a key role in the design and analysis of the pilot project, in particular in terms of understanding potential issues around societal uptake. The Round Tables also pointed to the need to identify an Arabic word or phrase for 'm-health', in order to make m-health part of everyday life.

Understanding the relationship between a person and their mobile phone, the ways that communicative practices are experienced as empowering, and how this can be integrated into health interventions that sustain autonomy and self-management, all demand what is known as 'qualitative research'. The Round Tables strongly urged us to integrate a social scientist with these skills into our team, and this remains a major challenge for us. The difficulties we have encountered in this area highlight the relative weakness of the social sciences in Iraq, and possibly more broadly in the MENA region, and the low-level of integration of the social sciences with medical and technical disciplines. The social sciences, for example, traditionally play little role in health programme design in the MENA region, as in Iraq. And the period of war and sanctions has isolated the social sciences just as much as other disciplines from international developments. As a result, in Iraqi universities there is little research memory and capacity in areas of qualitative research, in particular in new fields of research such as modes of communication or experiences of embodiment. The Regional Round Tables highlighted how much these are critical to the long-term success of m-health projects, and this emphasis was part of CARA's decision to develop a specific programme to strengthen links between the social sciences in Iraq and international developments, through a programme of regional Round Tables specifically dedicated to the social sciences in Iraq.

CHALLENGES AND POSSIBILITIES

By the end of 2011 we have developed the technical systems linking basic mobile phones with a glucometer, together with protocols for data transfer, management, security and access. These are important achievements, and we are now proceeding to the pilot study where we explore patient experience on the one hand, and the ways the data generated can become part of the management of diabetes. We will need to continue to attach a great importance to the technical dimensions of the study, and without these m-health will prove impossible. But at the same time we will need to focus on the human experiences of research participants on the one hand, and health professionals on the other, to grapple with the challenge we set ourselves at the outset of this project: namely, the development of self-management, where m-health becomes a medium where people can understand their diabetes better, and where we can ensure real change in the management of diabetes that will lead to real and lasting health outcomes.

This is a small pilot study, but one that opens up important possibilities. It highlights the importance of developing new types of interdisciplinary research in order to respond in a more holistic way to the challenge of health and illness, a central dimension of contemporary health policy. It underlines the importance of such research within Iraqi universities, as even though this is a small project, it has had implications in terms of university education that will eventually have an impact beyond our immediate universities. It also highlights the ways research can build new links between the university and its wider environment, highlighting the critical role of the university in rebuilding civil society. And this study has also highlighted the importance of a regional perspective, one that extends to the MENA region and to key relationships of international solidarity with scholars and universities beyond the region as such.

Our study also highlights important dimensions of CARA's Iraq Research Fellowship Programme. The IRFP aims at building links between Iraqi academics who have had to leave the country and universities and scholars both in Iraq and internationally. The IRFP thus opens up new networks and possibilities for scholars who have left the country, but also, through connecting Iraqi universities to international networks of scholarship, the programme is directly supporting the rebuilding of Iraqi universities, in particular their research capacity, from supporting awareness of current international research to the development of university governance and ethics infrastructure. As such, the CARA programme does not simply offer support to scholars who have left the country. It allows these scholars to be part of the urgent task of rebuilding the research capacity of Iraqi universities, and through this, to participating in the reconstruction of Iraqi society.

NOTE AND THANKS

The research team working on m-health and diabetes has involved a number of people, some of whom have changed over the two-year period. The team is led by Professor Robert Istepanian of the University of Kingston in London. Dr Alaa Musa Kuttar is a diabetologist at the University of Basra. Dr Karim Al-Jeboury is a software engineer teaching and researching in Amman, Jordan, while previously of the Baghdad University of Technology. Dr Gaia Shall of the University of Basra is a computer engineer working on mobile media and wireless networks. Professor Kevin McDonald, of Goldsmiths College in London and Victoria University in Melbourne, is a sociologist and a CARA Facilitator supporting the team. The project has greatly benefitted through the support of medical mentors, Dr Nazar Amso, Clinical Senior Lecturer in Obstetrics & Gynaecology at the School of Medicine at Cardiff University, and Professor John Gregory, Professor of Paediatric Endocrinology at the School of Medicine at Cardiff University. The wider project, in particular the Round Tables, have received precious support from Mr Ali Kubba, Consultant Gynaecologist at Guy's Hospital and St Thomas Hospital in London.

REFERENCES

Chesterman, S. (2001). *Civilians in War*, Boulder: Lynne Rienner.
Hamdan, Susan (2011). 'A big push to expand mobile service in Iraq', *New York Times*, 2 March, available at http://www.nytimes.com/2011/03/03/world/middleeast/03iht-M03B-ZAIN.html, accessed 1-12-11.
MENA Diabetes Leadership Forum (2010). *Dubai Declaration on Diabetes and Chronic Non-Communicable Diseases in the Middle East and North Africa (MENA) Region*, United Arab Emirates.
Nature Editorial (2010). Support refugee scientists, *Nature*, 4 November, Volume *468*, 5. Macmillan Publishers Limited.
UNFPA (2007).*State of World Population*, New York.
World Health Organization (2007).*Republic of Iraq: Iraq Family Health Survey Report*, Baghdad, WHO.

HEATHER BRUNSKELL-EVANS, KEVIN MCDONALD, MICHELE
MOORE AND ROGER SLEE

ASPIRATIONS FOR NEW POSITION, IDENTITY AND AGENCY: REIMAGINING RESEARCH FOR RECLAIMING THE ACADEMY IN IRAQ

In this concluding chapter, four facilitators of the IRFP, reflect not only on the contributions to the book but on the IRFP in general. Sarah Beazley, University of Manchester and Jason Sparks now at Konkuk University, Korea also served as occasional facilitators and their input to projects has also been recognised and valued.

The reader will have discerned that the chapters found in the book are very different from typical collections of research papers. Such collections typically present the results of research or scientific arguments, with much else to do with research process in the background not deserving of discussion, or at the least not treated as relevant to what is being argued or the data being presented. In this case, however, the chapters are surprisingly quite different. They recount experiences of research, efforts to build teams, struggles to find a home in the university, isolation from international research networks, the absence of resources to build robust research laboratories or programmes, and the micro-politics contingent on the unique experiences of academics in Iraq. Perhaps just as surprisingly not a single chapter uses the term 'refugee', despite academics who 'fit' this humanitarian category being members of each team. All the chapters explore experiences of displacement, trauma and at times danger and these experiences are at the heart of the attempts of the scholars to 're-imagine research'. As such, these contributions point more widely to the aims of the IRFP as it operates within the current context of CARA which, eighty years after its inception is also responding to the changing social and political landscape of the 21st Century.

REIMAGINING RESEARCH

What is most striking in the experiences recounted in this book is their urgency. Each team wants to engage with questions of great importance and develop research that brings about real transformation. One team of biomedical scientists confronts the significant growth of anti-biotic resistant strains of TB, another team sets out to explore the way theatre might be used as a tool to transform university environments shaped by violence and authoritarianism. One team sets out to explore the post-war experience of female academics and the significant

H. Brunskell-Evans & M. Moore (Eds.), Reimagining Research for Reclaiming the Academy in Iraq: Identities and Participation in Post-Conflict Enquiry: The Iraq Research Fellowship Programme, 89–97.

deterioration in their situation, another explores the reshaping of educational curricula and its impacts on schools post 2003. Yet another team sets out to explore ways that paediatric training recognises and responds to the trauma of war while another engages with the growing health crisis focused around diabetes.

Every chapter highlights risk. The simple decision to attend a play was identified by its audience as a potential source of danger. Being identified as a scholar with international networks is a potential source of marginalisation within the complex micro-politics of universities in Iraq. Developing a media profile through speaking out publicly about health risks or health policy, in many countries regarded as part of the normal role of a researcher, is experienced as making the person involved stand out as a potential target. In one case one of the researchers involved in the Programme makes a decision not to inform their university for fear of adverse consequences of being involved in an internationally supported research network. In another the simple fact of undertaking a period of training out of the country is perceived as bringing with it a risk of 'contamination'. Undertaking interviews, transporting samples and travelling to research sessions, all actions at times involving negotiation of checkpoints, are always undertaken with extreme caution. The scholars involved in the Fellowship are all deeply aware of the extent that academics, in particular publicly known academics, have been targeted by assassinations in the post-invasion period.

To this is coupled the extreme difficulty of experiencing agency, the sense that one can act and transform one's environment. These chapters describe the constant difficulty of making systems work and the extraordinary weight of organisational inertia. This highlights the extent to which universities remain government agencies, with their culture shaped by loyalty to leaders, whether political appointees, or at the worst post-2003 period, militia leaders. Such a university environment and the chaos surrounding it do not reward research that poses new questions.

The very attempt to undertake research in post-invasion Iraq has highlighted the absence of research ethics infrastructure and training in research ethics. In a context where the university is regarded as closely associated with those in power, what can 'informed consent' mean, with its emphasis on research participants freely consenting to be involved in research, and feeling free to withdraw at any time? This is compounded by the social distance that at times may separate researchers and the social groups involved in their research. The extent of difficulty associated with the practice of research was highlighted by the years of enforced isolation of Iraqi scholars during the long period of international sanctions preceding the 2003 invasion. The physical and technical sciences found themselves unable to import equipment and technology, access to scientific journals was severely limited, while the social and cultural sciences experienced an enforced marginalisation under an authoritarian regime where the many voices associated with public debate and experimentation were suppressed.

RECLAIMING THE ACADEMY

Despite this context, the majority of the research teams sought out and managed to find allies and supporters in their respective universities. In the process, they have served as catalysts for institutional change and capacity building. In a number of cases, university leaders have defended the research projects recognising the issues at stake such as the absence of ethics infrastructure or academic cultures that are untrusting of research or international contact, and have actively responded to the challenge of nourishing wider and deeper relationships as part of rebuilding the capacity of Iraqi universities. In some cases this has led to inter-university department initiatives that have been able to secure support through UK government funding mechanisms. In other cases university deans have directed financial and administrative support to the projects, aware of their importance in developing a research capacity in Iraqi universities. The transformation has thus extended beyond the research teams as such.

One important 'multiplier' effect of the projects has been the development of Regional Round Tables. These Round Tables have been an opportunity for Iraqi scholars to meet and develop links with researchers from other countries in the Middle East and North Africa (MENA) region, as well as extending possibilities for enlarging and strengthening networks between scholars in Iraq and Iraqi scholars living in exile. But these have not duplicated traditional academic conferences. Instead the Round Tables have been fora bringing together researchers with other 'change agents', from the representatives of the World Health Organization or technology companies who participated in the Round Table around Diabetes, to NGO and advocacy networks brought together in a Round Table that developed out of the Female Academics project. This pattern has been extended by a Round Table around the challenge of rebuilding the social sciences in the MENA region, a challenge made all the more urgent by the dramatic transformations at work in the region since 2011. The Round Tables highlight a critical dimension of reclaiming the academy: not only constructing functional research and teaching units and viable university governance, but developing a culture and practice of openness and engagement extending beyond national and academic boundaries.

All contributors to the book continue to carry out high quality, cutting edge research and dissemination. New transnational social and academic networks have transformed the international standing of work being done by Iraqi scholars. All IRFP teams have exploited new connections to enable wide public engagement with their research in interesting ways which map on to criteria for research 'excellence' in the UK (REF Consultation and Public Engagement, 2010). These include conference and seminar presentations, study visits, participation in on-line discussion fora, membership of academic societies, producing posters, academic writing and writing for other stakeholder audiences such as government ministries, advisory bodies, policy makers, practitioners and research users. New sources of funding have been applied for and gained. New cultures of research-led teaching are being cultivated in the universities of Iraq. New modes of research training and delivery are being pioneered as some teams promote their activity through the medium of television, film, performing arts, Ning, Facebook, Twitter and other social media. New engagements with scholarship are fostered through serendipity as an IRFP scholar introduces another Iraqi to a prospective research supervisor or Journal Editor they have met through the programme. Excitement and new energies have been created as the dynamics of partnership and team working become established; *'now I am glad to understand this project is team project not individual work and in this regards, hopefully sharing all the report and ideas between us, we will be able to success our goal ...every week we should prepare a report from article we read and exchange this reports'*.

New engagements with humanity have come about as individuals hear of and share in the stories circumstances of academics and their families in need of assistance *'it was gray and rainy in Manchester when the new Iraqi researcher arrived. I am not involved in her project but she sent me an email saying 'I am here 3 week ago'. She was terribly lonely so we met for lunch. She misses her family so'*. The IRFP through CARA has made multiple differences to post-conflict Iraq 'and Governments and other funders would do well to consider contributing to an expansion of such efforts' (Nature Editorial, 2010).

CREATIVITY, TRANSFORMATIONS AND TENSIONS

As we have seen, the core of the IRFP are the research teams made up of Iraqi researchers living both within and outside the country, co-ordinated by western principal investigators and facilitators. The workshops engaged with a range of themes, from wide-ranging debates about the challenges facing reconstructing university research in Iraq to sessions on research methods, accessing international scholarly resources, grant application writing or writing for scientific publication, strategies for accessing international research networks, and research ethics. Some of the most powerful debates were in effect the 'university in action', where scholars moved outside their disciplinary fields and discussed priorities and ideas with people working in very different ways: medical bio-scientists debating with educationalists, researchers working on gender debating with soil scientists. Several of the chapters in this book recount these exchanges. At one level they seem at first remote from the practical tasks that each research team was confronting, but at another level such encounters are at the very heart of what constitutes a university, where very different disciplines, paradigms and even ways of experiencing the world succeed in communicating with each other. All the chapters in this book recount a shift from experiences of mutual incomprehension, and even implicit uncertainty or mistrust, to a new sense of shared endeavour extending across disciplinary boundaries that many scholars in much better resourced universities would rarely attempt. These exchanges were without doubt critical moments in the Fellowship's 'reimagining' of what a university could be: a place of openness to new ways of experiencing and thinking about the world.

Several of the chapters in this book point to tensions at work in the research teams. Chapter Four details the experience of a participant who describes the first encounter with the IRFP as an experience of 'underlying distrust' regarding the capacity of Iraqi scholars to undertake 'valid research within Western criteria'. The source of what was experienced as distrust was considered in part a consequence of the absence of social science research methods in Iraq, and in part a result of western academics' lack of knowledge of Iraqi realities, in particular the difficulty of establishing a clear separation between 'policies' on the one hand and 'politics' on the other. This chapter suggests a degree of mutual incomprehension: with western scholars concerned that what should be research becoming instead an exercise in making a case for a political programme, while Iraqi scholars were concerned that they were confronting an expression of Western orientalism present in a stereotypical view of the lack of interest in accuracy characterising 'the oriental mind'.

Strong language used in this chapter captures several things. The first is the extent that the early period of the IRFP involved powerful experiences of incomprehension across academic cultures. These were equally evident in the exchanges that took place between social and cultural scientists on the one hand and natural scientists and technical disciplines on the other. This highlights a style of work that was not 'managed', but set out to explore challenges. This recurs in other chapters as well, for example in Chapter Five where a group of researchers set out to explore 'experiences of insufficiency'. At stake in all of these is the encounter with difference. Such an experience can be one that generates fear and closure, as appears increasingly evident as many countries attempt to close their borders. But the encounter with difference can also be one where we encounter our own experience of incompleteness, most directly addressed in the chapter exploring 'insufficiency'. We can be afraid of this kind of experience, or it can be central to our shared humanity. Much of the human experience that came to sustain the Iraq Fellowship, and that we see animating the chapters above, is the product of encounters that produced such a sense of shared humanity, one grounded in our incompleteness and insufficiency.

BEYOND THE 'REFUGEE' VERSUS 'EXILE' PARADIGM

One of the most striking features of the IRFP has been the absence of any evidence that the Iraqi scholars involved in the programme make sense of themselves in terms of categories such as 'refugee' or 'non-refugee'. At this point, while the programme is still underway, it is probably premature to seek to draw out all the implications of what may be at stake here, but it does highlight important questions for international humanitarian organisations working with displaced people.

Edward Said's classical distinction between the terms 'refugee' and 'exile' developed in his 'Reflections on exile' (Said 2000) is an important starting point to open out this question. The term 'exile', he notes, finds its origins in age-old practices of banishment, while the term 'refugee' is 'a creation of the twentieth-century state', a term suggesting 'large hordes of innocent and bewildered people requiring urgent international assistance'. The term 'exile', he suggests, carries with it 'a touch of solitude and spirituality', an on-going degree of isolation and displacement (2000: 181). Not only does the term not fit with the cultural world of the people involved in the IRFP, the term increasingly denies agency to those it is attached to, with the passivity of the refugee.

What is significant is that the Iraqi scholars involved in the programme use neither of these terms. None of those who 'objectively' correspond to the status of 'refugee' describe themselves as such in the chapters of this book, despite the IRFP programme being sponsored by an organization with the term in its title. In part this may highlight a critical aspect of the experience of the exile that Said explores, namely what he describes as the 'habit of dissimulation', a sense of living in different worlds leading to acting as if one is at home 'wherever one happens to be' (2000:181). This, implies Said with great perception, means that the exile will almost never describe himself or herself as homeless. To do so would undermine the principal response to the experience of displacement she or he is living. In Chapter Three Irada al-Jeboury describes enforced departure from one's country as *'another kind of death'*. The exile experience has been respected throughout the IRFP. Nobody has been labelled in ways that would be experienced as destructive or in ways that are not self-defined.

But this absence of the terms 'exile' and 'refugee' may also reflect the extent to which the IRFP has sought to embed itself within the culture and practices of the MENA region (with its regional office in Amman and its support programmes located in that city). Most of the Arab states that have provided refuge to Iraqis are not signatories to the 1951 United Nations Refugee Convention, and most of these States consider that the term 'refugee' is unsuitable to describe movements of people within the Arab world, with the exception of the Palestinian experience. In that sense, within the MENA region term 'refugee' refers to an experience of collective dispossession of territory and subsequent expulsion. Otherwise, where Arab states receive displaced people they will describe them as 'visitors' or 'guests', regardless of the reasons for their mobility (see Mason 2011). This use of the term 'guest' captures powerful cultures of hospitality, with important implications for the experience of Iraqis across the region (Mason 2011). This cultural pattern, where the term 'refugee' is more a term associated with international conventions than a term groups and individuals use to identify themselves or others, is reflected throughout the chapters in this book.

But the absence of this term may point towards a wider set of transformations concerning what it means to be a displaced person today. In a world of increasing interconnection and mobility, displacement is less and less lived as a single event, and is increasingly experienced as a process that may last months or years (Gill, Caletrio and Mason 2011). In this context there is not a clear and irreversible shift in status from one identity to another, while different types of mobility (professional, political, economic, religious) may overlap, with routes travelled not in a single, linear direction, but as fluid and volatile. The efforts of the Iraqi scholars described in this book, and their struggle to find words to capture this effort, is a politics of life. It is a politics with incomprehensions, uncertainties, and false beginnings but it is also a politics of possibility.

The IRFP sets out to foster agency and rebuild connections. This has been at the source of the powerful experiences of transformation that have been grappled with in the chapters above. The reader may have noted that on several occasions different writers have referred to the experience of engaging in research as 'strange'. This word captures the sense of risk and possibility, of an openness to dimension of experience that we cannot predict nor necessarily imagine. It captures realities and experiences that we may not have words to describe, that go beyond our current language.

This agency and openness has been at the centre of the IRFP, a programme that has tried to respect the cultural norms of the region and the increasingly complex lived experiences associated with displacement today. Rather than spending most of its funds in the United Kingdom, money and resources have been focused on supporting the efforts of people in Iraq, and rebuilding connections between scholars in the country, those outside the country, and international research networks. In this there has been a shared effort, not to turn away from a devastated Iraq, but to develop a programme to support displaced scholars, to direct resources to supporting clear and identifiable transformations in the country, reduce pressure on scholars to leave, open out paths of connection that will facilitate the eventual return of those who can, and ensure that those scholars who cannot do not find themselves cut off from the task of rebuilding their country.

CONCLUSION

One important aim for the book was that the Iraqi contributors would respond to questions about the actuality of what is involved in efforts to work collaboratively across Iraqi and Western academic cultures, across disciplinary boundaries, across the boundaries of ordinary human existence as scholars came to build projects with academics from far safer life contexts, not typically wrought by state fragility, regional insecurity and threat to personal and professional identity and survival. Looking back on this brief, and on the willingness of contributors to dive into it, provides testimony to the vision of CARA and the power of the IRFP.

We have found through the chapters that it is possible for collaborative research in the context of post-conflict Iraq to engage with multiple voices, ideas, practices and aspirations. All research teams have struggled to realise and promote a wealth of possibilities for forging new landscapes of enquiry that will bridge agendas for rebuilding Higher Education in Iraq and rebuilding peace and social justice. Diverse research interests, experiences and observations have been presented which consistently reveal deeply held uncertainty about ways of researching but which also serve to pin-down fortitude and optimism about the possibilities of cross-cultural research as a key driver of change in post-conflict Iraq.

Different conceptualizations of research are evident through the pages of this book as the link between research and the future of Iraq is explored. Recurring anxieties have emerged across the chapters; perceptions of injustice and oppression within research practice itself surface which affirm the critical importance of readiness to completely re-imagine research practice. Authors make plain the importance of valuing and celebrating Iraqi knowledge and perspectives. They have not been afraid to expose practical problems, conceptual confusion, vastly different assumptions about the nature of research and transgressive thinking embedded in their work. Discernible shifts in understandings of research convey constantly changing images of the power of research for rebuilding Iraq. Arguably, these have grown through the assembly of scholars enabled by the IRFP with its subtle insistence on mixing up the multiple voices of those who aspire to build research, transform the academy and rebuild Iraq.

By 2012, despite some of the political and religious differences between and within the research groups we can report there is a growing atmosphere of trust which pervades our collective work on the IRFP. We acknowledge the complexity of evolving starting points for meaningful change in the Iraqi academic context; we also applaud the concerted energy and enthusiasm of all IRFP contributors, in the absence of any previous model, to mobilise the task of bringing about a successful programme. This book has taken the story of participation in IRFP as its central focus and through these stories we have tried to identify a modus operandi for better research, for better rebuilding of academy in post conflict situations that is perhaps informed by the struggles we have taken with each step forward.

The editors have made no attempt in the chapters to dilute the reality of the pain embedded in the experience of Iraqi scholars and researchers. There have been casualties, of which this is only one example:

> *Finally some sense [about the disappearance of an Iraqi scholar] ...they have banned him from the university as unfit to work and closed his university account whilst enlisting him on a support programme so that he can get some help with what they are diagnosing as mental health problems.*

Despite very high potential of all projects at the start there have been disappointments along the way, such as when plans for an IRFP conference had to be shelved. There have been routine moments of despair:

> *Dears,*
> *I very sorry today to hear that my request to get Visa to Amman has not accepted.*
> *I am very depressed. My hope was to see all of you and to meet our PI.*
> *Ok. Please inform me what will happen with you and what I should do.*

But new transnational networks of support have come into play, as described earlier, as a way of ensuring the participation of Iraqi scholars in research. These also offer personal support and help to reduce the risk of marginalisation Iraqi researchers contend with, as an Iraqi researcher in exile replies to her Iraq bound research partner:

> *oh, I am so sorry to hear this news, why they didn't give you visa is there is any reasons? We hope to see you again. Don't worry I will forward to you all the information inshalla.*
> *Your sister in the IRFP*

It is in the recognition and understanding of the struggle of Iraqi scholars that possibilities for reconciliation, for the repopulation of the academy, and for the rebuilding of research that will reveal new landscapes and horizons for enquiry, that possibilities open up for an inclusive academy in Iraq, in which academics are free from tyranny and oppression will be able to grow. Of course there is no room for complacency. The book's strengths lie in the extraordinary willingness of contributors to share together and then describe for public consumption their experience as IRFP scholars. Each chapter has provided vivid insights into the conditions in which Iraqi researchers find themselves and incisive overview and analysis of what is involved in beginning the process of shifting the conditions which threaten to limit the repopulating of the academy. Yet for many, the requirement for personal reflection is wholly unfamiliar within their discipline, their workplace or their culture and the process of personal exposure is not without risk as writers have said.

Through their willingness to engage in critical self-reflection of their experience of involvement in the IRFP, Iraqi scholars make clear their commitment to rebuilding academy in Iraq. Hopes and frustrations, successes and confusion even devastation but also great celebration, have been made plain. The chapters reflect how contributors feel about their position, identity and agency in the process of rebuilding the academy. We hope that the impact of the IRFP and of what we have all learned will open up new platforms for those who are serious about rebuilding Iraq and that its sponsorship by CARA will have enduring consequences.

REFERENCES

Gill, N., Caletrio, J. & Mason, V. (2011) 'Introduction: Mobilities and forced migration', *Mobilities,* 6, 3, 301–316.

Mason, V. (2011) 'Theim/mobilities of Iraqi refugees in Jordan: Pan-Arabism, 'Hospitality' and the figure of the refugee', *Mobilities,* 6, 3, 353–373.

Nature Editorial (2010). Support refugee scientists, *Nature,* 4 November, Volume *468,* 5. Macmillan Publishers Limited.

REF *Consultation and Public Engagement* (2010) National Coordinating Centre for Public Engagement http://www.publicengagement.ac.uk/how-we-help/event-reports/ref-workshop (accessed 6/12/11).

Said, E (2000) *Reflections On Exile and Other Essays*, Harvard, Harvard University Press.

Lightning Source UK Ltd.
Milton Keynes UK
UKOW050723141012

200553UK00002B/2/P